Attachment-Focused Parenting

ATTACHMENT-FOCUSED PARENTING

Effective Strategies to Care for Children

DANIEL A. HUGHES

W.W. NORTON & COMPANY

New York · London

For information about permission to reproduce
selections from this book, write to
Permissions, W. W. Norton & Company, Inc.,
500 Fifth Avenue, New York, NY 10110

For information about special discounts for bulk purchases,
please contact W. W. Norton Special Sales at
specialsales@wwnorton.com or 800-233-4830.

Composition by Bytheway Publishing Services
Manufacturing by R.R. Donnelley-Bloomsburg
Production Manager: Leeann Graham

Library of Congress Cataloging-in-Publication Data

Hughes, Daniel A.
   Attachment-focused parenting : effective strategies to care for
children / Daniel A. Hughes. — 1st ed.
      p.   cm. — (A Norton professional book)
   Includes bibliographical references and index.
   ISBN 978-0-393-70555-3 (hardcover)
   1. Attachment behavior in children.   2. Parent and child.
   3. Parenting.   I. Title.
BF723.A75H84   2009
649'.1—dc22   2008038563

ISBN 13: 978-0-393-70555-3

W. W. Norton & Company, Inc., 500 Fifth Avenue,
New York, N. Y. 10110
www.wwnorton.com
W. W. Norton & Company Ltd., Castle House, 75/76 Wells St.,
London W1T 3QT

4   5   6   7   8   9   0

To my granddaughter,
Alice Rose Thibodeau

CONTENTS

ACKNOWLEDGMENTS

Numerous researchers have been working for over 50 years to help us in our understanding of the central role of attachment and intersubjectivity in human development. They are far too many to acknowledge and I will mention only a few who have been most instrumental in my developing knowledge. They are Alan Sroufe, Dante Chichetti, Mary Dozier, John Bowlby, and Colwyn Trevarthen. I am also most grateful to two theorists who have taken this research, along with research in other fields, and have begun to suggest connections in many applied fields. They are Allan Schore and Dan Siegel, who have supported my own work at many times and in many ways.

I wish to also acknowledge how indebted I am to my friends, who have enabled me to understand attachment and intersubjectivity in a way that I could never comprehend simply from reading books or attending conferences. Through this work I have become friends with colleagues throughout the US, Canada, UK, Ireland, and Australia. Who they are and what they bring to their work continues to influence my own professional and personal development.

My parents and siblings have been part of my safety and intersubjective experience over my whole life's journey. My three daughters have taught me—and continue to teach me—at least as much as I have taught them. Most recently I have discovered these realities from the perspective of a grandfather. Alice Rose does not yet know it, but she too is teaching me, possibly most of all at this time of my life. And so, this book is dedicated to her.

Attachment-Focused Parenting

Connection versus Correction

Although he remembered that his mother said that he needed to do his chore before he could watch TV, 9-year-old John turned on the TV before finishing the chore. He broke the rule, and if someone asked him why he did so, most likely he would say, without much thought, "I wanted to watch the show." If he thought more about the event, he would still be likely to simply say, "I just wanted to watch it."

The meaning of the situation for the boy is likely to change if his mother discovers his behavior and responds to it. Her thoughts and feelings will further develop his own impressions about his behavior. If she experiences it as an act of disobedience, he is likely to experience himself as being disobedient. If she sees it as a sign of laziness, he is likely to think that he is lazy. If she thinks that he is selfish because he places his own wishes above her expectations, he is likely to see himself as selfish. Similarly, he might become sneaky, defiant, or disrespectful if that was his mother's experience of the event.

The meaning of the situation would be still different for the boy if his mother experienced it less negatively. If she saw it as not uncommon for a 9-year-old child to disregard a minor expectation, he would experience it as an aspect of routine childhood behaviors. If she thought that he had a difficult day and wanted to relax for a little while before doing his chore, then most likely he would experience his motive as being similar. In either example, he will not experience any negative messages about himself that his behavior came to represent.

Another possibility is that his mother will note her son's behavior and not make any assumptions about his reasons for it. She might think that its meaning lies in the thoughts, feelings, wishes, and intentions that underlie the behavior without knowing what they might be. She remains nonjudgmental about his motives while simply observing the behavior. She will then decide whether to respond to it or not. Or she might explore with him what his motives might have been before deciding how to respond. She does not attach meaning to the behavior, but rather becomes engaged with her son to understand its meaning. Since he may not know why he did what he did, this engagement may help them both to understand together what the behavior represents. Thus they might have the following dialogue:

> *Mom*: I notice that you haven't finished putting away your stuff.
> *John*: I know, Mom, but I'll do it when the show is over.
> *Mom*: We spoke about your getting the stuff put away first. Any sense as to why you didn't get it done before turning on the TV? You had enough time.
> *John*: I know, Mom. I was reading my book and didn't notice the time.
> *Mom*: Okay, John, you can watch the end of the show. Then finish your chore. Then you have to tell me about the book you are reading. It must really be interesting!

In this example, John's mother decided that his interest in the book and the TV show were strong and as a result he had not left enough time to finish his chore. She might have further thought that he seldom broke rules and that her decision to allow him to finish watching the show would not encourage him to break more rules in the future. His reasons, namely his dual interests and limited time, made sense to her and most likely elicited a more flexible response than if she thought that he was deliberately testing her authority. If she noticed a pattern developing, she might have said that she would now expect him to get permission from her to watch the show before finishing the chore. If he failed to do so, she might then turn off the show until the chore was finished. If that was not sufficient, she might say that he must miss the show that day, or even the next day too.

However, John's mother might decide that he is disregarding her rules but still choose to avoid providing escalating consequences. She might, instead, explore with him his motives for his apparently deliberate testing of her authority:

Mom: John, I've told you a few times now that you need to ask me for permission before watching TV if your chores are not done, but you turned it on again. What's up?

John: I don't know. I just feel like it!

Mom: Sounds like you feel strongly about it. What makes it so hard for you to follow that rule?

John: I'm not a baby! Asking permission to watch TV is stupid!

Mom: You sure have a lot of anger about it. Must be hard if you think that I'm treating you like a baby.

John: Well, you are! I'm 9, not 2!

Mom: And as you get older you think that you should be able to do what you want. And not have to do what I say, like getting your chores done first.

John: Yeah. Why do I have to do them anyway?

Mom: As you get older, it seems like you think I shouldn't be able to tell you what you can do and not do.

John: Yeah, it does.

Mom: I hear you, son. This is an important, but difficult, part of growing up. And you and I are going to have some differences about what you can do and not do. We'll get through them. Right now I do want you to do your chores before watching TV and to ask permission if you haven't finished them. I know that you don't like that but I still think it is important enough to have you do it.

John: I don't like it.

Mom: I know you don't, John. I get that. Because you're getting older, you're more clear about what you want and don't want. And I think that's a good thing, though we will disagree at times.

John: Okay. I'll turn off the dumb show! But I don't think it's fair!

Mom: I understand. Thanks for doing it anyway. And I do
   know that you are certainly not a baby any longer. You can
   handle so many things so well now. It's like you learn to do
   some new things everyday. Way to go!

In this sequence, when John was testing his mother's authority, she
openly explored his motives with him and he was able to realize that
he thought that as he matured he would increasingly be able to decide what to do. He was beginning to think that simply doing what he
was told was a sign that he was still a baby. His mother was able to
support this emerging awareness, see its value in his development,
acknowledge that it would lead to conflicts between them, be confident that their relationship was strong enough to manage the conflicts, and still tell him to follow the rule. She evaluated his behavior
but not his inner life that led to his behavior. In so doing, she pre-
served her role in helping him to organize his experience of the
events of his life, including his own behavior and her response. After
hearing his mother differentiate his inner life from his behavior, John
was much more ready to accept her authority over his behavior while
still experiencing himself as an increasingly autonomous older child.

In this example, John's mother's response varies depending upon
her perception of the reasons for the behavior and its frequency and
importance, as well as John's response to her at each step of the exchange. If she chooses to address his behavior, then she explores
his possible motives through nonjudgmental curiosity. In so doing,
she is respecting his developing sense of self and her role in nurturing
its development.

Attachment theory and research have convincingly taught us that our
children are much more than the sum of their behaviors, and that our
understanding of them and our relationships with them rely on much
more than evaluating their behaviors. Attachment theory suggests that
knowledge of a child begins from the inside out, and that such developing knowledge is fundamental to our emerging relationship with him.

I have been a therapist for children and their parents for over 30
years. During much of that time, I have worked with children who

experienced abuse and neglect within their homes and who, as a result, lost the readiness and even the ability to trust and learn from their foster or adoptive parents. To understand and help these children, I have followed the teachings of those who have studied attachment and its role in human development. As I found ways to reach these children, I also developed a much more comprehensive appreciation for how attachment-focused research can guide all parents in their efforts to better raise their children. From the narrow perspective of a therapist focusing on children whose attachment relationships are the most damaged, I have gradually come to focus on the nature of these relationships themselves and their implications for child rearing. My clinical practice has also reflected this shift in that I now provide attachment-focused treatment to all families, rather than foster and adoptive families only (Hughes, 2007).

This book is written to be a guide for all parents and a resource for all mental health clinicians and parent educators who are searching for ways to effectively love, discipline, and communicate with children, whether they are 3, 7, 13, or 17. It describes ways to set limits, provide guidance, and manage the responsibilities and difficulties of daily life, while at the same time communicating safety, fun, joy, and love. The theory and research that primarily emerged through the study of children from birth to age 4 has clear application to all children from infancy through late adolescence.

We are entering a new era regarding our understanding of how the human brain is designed to work in good relationships, and how such relationships are central to the cognitive, emotional, social, behavioral, and even biological development of the person. Nowhere is this emerging knowledge more evident than in the parent-child attachment relationship. Nowhere are the practical implications of this knowledge more important than in child-rearing decisions and recommendations. This work is one effort to build a bridge from the vast body of knowledge emerging from neuroscience and child development research to child-rearing principles and interventions.

At the core of successful parenting practices and optimal child development is the child's secure attachment relationship with his or her parents. This reality has often been overlooked, much as a fish overlooks water, in favor of theories that stress the importance of rewards and consequences for childhood behaviors to facilitate parents' influence over their child's development. This has been thought to be a straight-forward, one-directional process, whereby a child's good behavior would increase when it was followed by a positive consequence chosen by the parents. Other behaviors were thought to decrease if they were followed by either no consequence or a negative one. The relational context in which such consequences were applied was often overlooked in early behavioral programs. Later efforts attempted to define the parent-child relationship within the same learning theory that stressed the parents' reinforcing opportunities and abilities. By doing so, the rich and comprehensive reciprocal relationship and interpersonal learning that exists between parent and child were often overlooked.

The parent-child attachment relationship is the pivotal environmental factor in the child's development. It is the connection between the parent and child that is central to his development, not the corrections that are applied. Connection—not correction—is repeatedly able to guide a child in a positive manner without sacrificing his autonomy and individuality. Successful parenting continuously strives to find the balance between independence and dependence, freedom to choose and following the rules, autonomy and emotional intimacy, and maintaining safety and seeking to explore. By focusing on the parent-child relationship, one is able to best find the most appropriate balance for the individual child.

A book on raising children would be much easier to write if we could say that at a certain age, in a certain situation, parents should always respond to their child's behavior in one specific way. A compilation of such behaviors could become the parental text to keep handy for review in a difficult situation. However, such a book would necessarily ignore fundamental factors in the nature of an effective parent-child relationship and attachment security. These factors involve the necessity of the parent knowing the meaning of the behavior before knowing how best to respond to it. Such meaning involves the thoughts, feelings, wishes, intentions, perceptions, values, and memories associated with the behavior.

Finding the meaning of the behavior, along with the most appropriate response, requires that there be a reciprocal relationship between parent and child. The child's response continuously guides the parent to choose to modify, fine-tune, or even completely change a prior decision.

Within the parent-child relationship—as in all relationships—it is the reciprocal influence that each one has on the other that contributes to the success of the relationship. By allowing her child to influence her, a parent's authority is not diminished; rather, the parent is wiser, more effective, and more accepted by the child. Because of the nature and presence of this fine-tuning, when a parent allows the child to contribute to her decisions, the parent becomes attuned with her child, which enables the intervention to be both helpful in the given situation and also beneficial to the developing relationship. It is this reciprocal dance of the experience of the parent and child of each other that enables the interaction to be helpful in dealing with the current situation. The child learns as much from his ability to influence his parent's guidance of his behavior as he does from the guidance itself. The child has a role in determining what the guidance is. His inner life is important in assisting his parent to decide what is in his best interests. His inner life is a part of her inner life.

By being responsive to the child's response to her directive, the parent is able both to provide a directive that is most suitable to the situation and also to facilitate the child's ability to self-direct. Rather than seeking compliance, the parent is providing an alliance in which her perspective and experience contribute to the success of the child's actions but do not control these actions. Within this context, the parent and child develop a cooperative stance toward discovering the most appropriate manner of dealing with a situation. Within a framework that is influenced by attachment theory and research, discipline actually serves to strengthen both the parent-child relationship and the child's own developmental skills.

But parenting, and especially attachment-focused parenting, is much more than guidance and discipline. The context in which such interactions facilitate development and relationship enhancement is one of safety, comfort, support, and reciprocal enjoyment and sharing.

Such a context enables the child to experience a depth of confidence and commitment that enables all experiences, especially parent-child experiences, to become assimilated and integrated into a developing sense of self. Such experiences provide the child with a core sense of worth, of being loved, and of being able to love in turn. They provide an active stance of openness and exploration that generates momentum for the child to discover himself and his world, especially the world of his family.

The role of parents is to give their children life, and then to give them the opportunity to develop a life that balances autonomy and intimacy while deriving deep meaning and purpose from each. In attachment-focused parenting, the parent uses the unique knowledge that emerges from her relationship with her child as a guide to child rearing. The moment-to-moment attuned dance that a parent and child find themselves engaged in is a source of enjoyment and delight, as well as a source of awareness and understanding about each other's thoughts, feelings, and intentions. This awareness is the best guide to knowing what is best for our children and for our relationships with our children. This book attempts to describe the nature of this relationship-based knowledge and the factors that are central to its development.

For the sake of clarity, when referring to a parent, "she" is the pronoun used unless referring specifically to the father. Also, "he" is the pronoun for the child unless referring specifically to a girl. Using "she" and "he" makes it easier to differentiate parent from child in the discussion. This is in no way intended to minimize the equal importance of the father in his child's development nor the relevance of this work for girls.

> *Love your child*
> *by learning the song that is in her heart*
> *and singing it to her*
> *when she forgets it.*
> —Anonymous

CHAPTER ONE

What Is Attachment and How Does Parenting Affect It?

In understanding the nature of the parent-child relationship and the pivotal role of attachment, we are able to see its impact on a child's emotional, cognitive, social, communicative, and even physiological and neurological development. Similarly, although possibly less obviously, we are also able to understand how being a parent affects the parent's development as well.

Some Background on Attachment

The "founding parents" of attachment theory and research are Mary Ainsworth and John Bowlby. They considered attachment to be characterized by six components, five of which were shared by other affectional bonds. The attachment relationship is:

1. Persistent or ongoing, not temporary
2. Directed toward a specific person
3. Emotionally significant
4. Directed toward maintaining contact with the other
5. Characterized by distress during periods of involuntary separation

6. Characterized by seeking security and comfort (This component is considered to be uniquely necessary for attachment [Cassidy, 1999, p. 12]).

While these six qualities might seem like common sense, they need to be stated because they are often taken for granted, and in the process may not influence child rearing as much as one might hope. Families are increasingly characterized by change, in the form of moves and loss of regular contact with extended family and friends, as well as divorce and blended families. With both parents often working long hours outside the home, the amount of time they are engaged in reciprocal and enjoyable activities with their children is likely to be less and the separations from their children longer. As the pressures on the parent-child relationship increase, the pressure to minimize its importance and focus on behavior also increases. Such behavioral focuses are appealing in the ease of application but often disappointing in their results.

It is also interesting to ask why these six qualities in relationships are important for human development. Why does the child need to have unique parents with whom to relate over time, rather than having parents in the present interchangeable with different ones in the future? Why should the contact be repetitive and lead to safety and comfort when together, along with distress during periods of separations? Why—and just as important, how—do our attachment figures become the source of our learning and discoveries about ourselves and our world? In answering these questions, we get a sense of how a child's development is intimately interwoven with the nature of his relationship with his parents.

A relationship that is characterized by attachment security facilitates many areas of development in the child. These include physiological and emotional regulation, self-reliance, resilience, social competence with peers, empathy for others, symbolic play, problem solving, intellectual development, communication and language skills, and self-integration and self-worth. The effects of attachment security on these areas of development are evident at the preschool stage, but also throughout childhood, adolescence, and into adulthood, as long as there were no significant disruptions in the security of the attachment relationships (Cassidy & Shaver, 1999; Grossman, Grossmann, & Waters, 2005; Sroufe, Egeland, Carlson, & Collins, 2005).

About two-thirds of all children manifest attachment security and are able to benefit from its positive influence on their development. The other third have attachments characterized by insecurity. The majority of children with insecure attachments still have organized patterns of attachment, though the patterns are limited in their benefit to the child and leave them vulnerable to some developmental challenges. By "organized" I mean that the child will manifest a fairly predictable series of responses to his attachment figures when he is in distress. In one pattern—*organized, but avoidant*—the child tends to minimize the importance of his parents in his development and overemphasizes his self-reliance skills. Failures and distress that might be managed and more easily reduced are more prevalent because such children avoid turning to their attachment figures when their engagement would be very beneficial. In the other pattern—*organized, but ambivalent*—the child overemphasizes his reliance on his parents and minimizes the need to develop his self-reliance skills. Such children often manage life's difficulties poorly because they do not develop the self-reliance skills needed to manage situations when their parents are not present. In essence, the first group stresses independence at the expense of relationships and the second group stresses relationships at the expense of independence. Neither is able to find the balance between the two that the securely attached child and adult can. The research is very clear that securely attached children do not become dependent on others as adults. If you meet your child's need to feel safe, your child will develop excellent self-reliance skills and resiliency while still being able to rely on significant others when the situation calls for it.

There is a final group of children with insecure attachments to their parents who do not manifest an organized pattern of attachment-related behaviors when in distress. These children are considered to have a *disorganized attachment*. They are neither able to successfully rely on themselves nor on their parents in any consistent way. They tend to be unpredictable in their response to stress. They tend to try to rigidly control the events of their lives in order to create some sense of safety by avoiding stressful events, since they are lacking in self-reliance and relationship skills that might manage such events. These children not only lack the positive benefits of attachment security, they are also at risk for developing many psychological problems in childhood and adulthood, ranging from aggression to short attention span and hyperactivity, conduct disorders and other behavioral problems, as well as anxiety, depression, and dissociation (Greenberg, 1999; Lyons-Ruth & Jacobvitz, 1999; Sroufe et al., 2005).

Secure attachment is the organizing principle of the parent-child relationship that I focus on in this book. It is also the organizing principle of the developing person.

Concepts Related to Attachment

This book looks at the parent-child relationship from a broader perspective than do some attachment researchers. Safety as well as exploration are central components in the parent-child relationship, and both are heavily influenced by attachment. To quote Grossman, Grossman, and Zimmermann:

> When their adaptation is challenged, secure (attached) children can flexibly explore possible solutions or perspectives while retaining a secure feeling during exploration, and if their competence is depleted, they can rely on and summon social resources. We have called this a "wider view of attachment," in which the freedom to explore in the face of adversity and the freedom to call for and accept help are both necessary and important aspects of security. (1999, p. 761)

Colwyn Trevarthen (2001) expands the parent-child relationship beyond safety when he speaks of the need of the infant for "joyful dialogic companionship" with his parents (p. 100). He refers to the attuned interactions between parent and infant as being central for development: "A major change in brain theory now gives emotions and their interpersonal transmission a regulatory role in both brain growth and cognitive mastery of experience" (p. 98). Trevarthen and others have stressed that our discovery of how infants develop in close intersubjective relationships with their parents leads to a new awareness of how parents might best guide the development of their children. The old understanding suggested that parents need to "constrain impulsive self-serving actions of children" through "instructive or corrective actions" so that they become "more socially responsible" (p. 99). Research on early childhood development now suggests that children need "a primary sharing of subjective impulses behind conscious experience and intentions" (p. 99). This research indicates that parents are wise to walk with, rather than stand above, their children while guiding them through developmental processes that will lead to a coherent life.

The intersubjective process that is referred to throughout this book is essentially a communication between parent and child whereby, through sharing their experiences, the inner lives of both child and parent are being deepened, expanded, and organized into more coherent selves. This communication process is nonverbal initially but eventually includes verbal processes as well. It is reciprocal. The parent will have the best influence on her child when her child is able to also have an influence on her. This communication process is crucial for successful development:

> The expressive-receptive channel of communication for mind processes has a special importance for an infant, when growth of brain and body are most rapid. Elaborate intuitive behaviors on both sides facilitate communication between infant and adult caregiver, and when there is a fault in either one, the infant is unable to benefit from care, and its psychological development will be affected. (Trevarthen, 2001, p. 98)

Dan Siegel (1999) has integrated much of the work of Trevarthen and others and demonstrated that what we are learning about attachment and development in infancy is equally true throughout life. Siegel believes that the essence of secure attachment involves the parent's ability to sensitively respond to the signals of the infant about his inner life and to communicate—essentially nonverbally—with the infant (p. 70).

Siegel devotes much of his work to describing how this shared, contingent communication between two individuals facilitates brain development for numerous emotional, cognitive, social, behavioral, and moral abilities. The need for this nonverbal, attuned communication persists throughout childhood, adolescence, and adulthood. With maturity, words tend to dominate the sharing of information, but the nonverbal foundation of the relationship remains pivotal if the communication is to lead to a deep and meaningful understanding and influence between those engaged with each other.

While the role of attachment has become increasingly evident in thousands of studies in the various fields of child development, more recently its central place is also becoming apparent in neurological research emerging from the new technologies for studying the structure and function of the brain. With these advances in brain research, there is increasing evidence that the brain is organized to be in attachment relationships, and such relationships are crucial for basic— and optimal—brain development (Schore, 2000). When an infant and his parent are engaged in attuned, intersubjective, nonverbal dialogue, crucial areas of the infant's brain within the prefrontal cortex are developing and becoming organized. Such developments do not occur when the infant is alone. This area of the brain is crucial for central areas of our functioning including affect regulation, social cognition, empathy, response flexibility, self-awareness, and fear modulation (Siegel, 1999). These and other related findings in brain research demonstrate that attachment security is crucial for many areas of optimal development in the child (Schore, 2000, 2003, 2005).

Throughout this work, communication between parent and child is seen as being the core of the relationship, beginning when the infant is in the arms of the parent and ending when the parent—on her deathbed—is in the arms of her child. Through the parent's nonverbal and verbal communication with her child, she opens her mind and heart to him, letting him know centrally that he exists within her inner life. She openly shares her thoughts and feelings, wishes and intentions, perceptions and memories with him, knowing that he will be safe with her perceptions of him. She is confident that when he becomes aware of anger directed toward his behavior, he will remain safe, knowing that the relationship will easily be repaired since the anger was not directed toward his inner self.

In the same manner, the parent actively facilitates the child's readiness and ability to reflect on his own inner life and share it with her. She communicates that his inner life is safe with her. It will not be judged; it will be accepted. In fact, he is safe if he allows her to explore his mind and heart with him, discovering qualities that are emerging or which had been concealed. Her presence in his inner life will enable him to regulate any intense emotions and to make sense of events that have been frightening or shameful.

Defining the Terms

Attachment refers to the child's relationship with the parent, rather than the parent's relationship with the child. Being securely attached to his parent, he turns to her for safety and support. She does not turn to her child for safety and support but rather to her partner, her own parents, or her friends. As the terms are used in this book, parents have an affectional bond with their child but are not attached to him.

Intersubjectivity refers to the process whereby the subjective experience of each member of a pair influences the subjective experience of the other. Through joining with the subjective experiences of their parents, children are able to regulate their own states and discover central qualities of their inner lives as well as the inner lives of their parents. Within such intersubjective experiences, the child develops the process of organizing and deepening his thoughts and feelings, perceptions and memories, wishes and intentions, values and beliefs. His parents' experience of him greatly influences his developing experience of himself. His parents' experience of the events and objects of his world greatly influence the manner by which he begins to experience these events and objects.

In this work, *affect* is defined as the nonverbal expression of one's emotional state. Affect is demonstrated in one's facial expressions, voice prosody (tone, speed, inflections, pitch, intensity), gestures, and posture. According to Dan Stern, a theorist and researcher, affect can be measured according to its intensity, rhythm, beat, contour, shape, and duration. Specific emotions have their unique affective expressions. It is quite easy to tell if a person is experiencing anger, fear, or happiness by observing the affective expression in his face, voice and gestures. Communicating an emotion primarily involves demonstrating its unique affective expression.

The distinction between an emotion and its affective expression is very important for two reasons. First, when a parent matches her child's affective expression of an emotion, without feeling the emotion herself, her child will experience acceptance, understanding, and empathy. When she matches her child's facial expression, voice prosody, and gestures, he will sense: "she gets it!" Second, when a parent matches the affect of the child, the child's affective state is being coregulated. If a child's emotion is becoming extreme, and his parent matches the affective expression of the emotion without feeling the emotion herself, the child's affect (and the underlying emotion) is likely to become less extreme and remain regulated. This difference is explained further in Chapters 3 and 7.

A child may convey anger in his voice, face, and gestures when he shouts, "I don't want to clean my room now!" A parent may respond with a similar nonverbal expression of affect, matching the intensity and rhythm of his voice and his unique facial expression, "You don't want to clean it now! You'd rather play with your friends!" But the parent's affective expression is of her child's emotional state, not her own. She is not angry. Rather she is conveying acceptance, understanding and empathy for his wish not to clean his room, which he is communicating through his affective expression of his angry emotion. His anger is much less likely to escalate when his affective expression is being matched. This affective matching is called "attunement" and it will be in evidence frequently throughout this book.

Reflective functioning refers to a specific form of thinking whereby the focus is on our inner life as well as the inner lives of others. Through reflecting, we become aware of the thoughts, emotions, wishes, intentions, perceptions, values, and memories that led to a behavior. Through enhanced reflective functioning, the child is better able to understand why he did something as well as why his parents did something too.

Central Principles of Attachment-Focused Parenting

Any consideration of attachment-focused parenting must begin by giving attention to safety and its central role in development. *Safety* refers to the general felt sense of safety rather than actual physical safety only. Without the experience of safety, children—and their parents as well—will become limited in their ability to develop their overall resources and to determine the best possible response to a given situation. Safety is explored in Chapter 2.

Chapter 3 focuses on understanding intersubjectivity. This word, which is not yet well known, attempts to describe how the core of emotional, social, cultural, and much practical knowledge develops and deepens when a child is able to experience his parents' experience. This process is very evident when observing how infants learn from their parents. This book will hopefully demonstrate why it is equally important in facilitating such learning for older children as well.

Attachment researchers have found that the most important predictor of a child's attachment patterns is the attachment patterns of his parents. This connection as well as its implications for child rearing is explored in Chapter 4.

When attachment security is maintained, there is a vital connection between the inner life of the child and the inner life of the parent. Chapter 5 focuses on an attitude that serves to facilitate this connection. This attitude has four components that tend to facilitate the child's affective and reflective skills within a context of both safety and exploration: playfulness, acceptance, curiosity, and empathy (PACE).

Chapter 6 focuses on the core communication patterns that facilitate both attachment security and intersubjectivity. The same patterns are evident between parent and infant and are centered upon reciprocal nonverbal expressions that convey both interest in and understanding of each other's inner life. Such communications more closely resemble storytelling dialogue than giving lectures and advice.

In Chapter 7, the importance of emotional development and its close ties with the affectional bonds referred to earlier is considered.

Skills involved in identifying, regulating, and expressing specific emotions and general affective state emerge within a relationship where such skills are valued and where the parent has achieved a high level of comparable skill development.

A child's emotional development is enhanced when he is also able to develop his reflective skills. This enables him to make sense of the immediate situation as well as his overall life path (i.e., his autobiographical narrative) and so organize it better. The integration of both affective and reflective skill development is of great benefit to the developing child, and parents can play an active role in helping their child develop reflection. Reflective skills are the topic of Chapter 8.

Chapter 9 focuses on the need to repair the parent-child relationship following conflicts, separations, misunderstandings, discipline, or periods of being unavailable. Such relationship breaks are a natural part of any ongoing relationship and their repair is necessary if the child is to have the confidence necessary to develop attachment security with his parents.

Finally, Chapter 10 focuses on understanding serious problems that may be associated with failures to establish attachment security and providing means to facilitate the resolution of these problems and repair of the relationship. When significant attachment problems emerge, there is a great risk that a downward spiral will develop that creates intensifying conflicts and problems. When the attachment relationship can be strengthened, these problems can be addressed with an increased likelihood of success.

These principles can be applied to all children, from infancy through late adolescence. The applications will certainly look different based on the age of the child, but the core principles, derived from how the brain functions and how all aspects of learning and development occur, are relevant for all ages.

CHAPTER TWO

Establish Safety

Safety is the springboard of family life and human development. This is the foundation of attachment theory, but it is often overlooked or taken for granted by other theories. Without physical safety, obviously we would not have the opportunity to live to maturity. Without a sense of safety, the ability to develop so as to reach our potential is greatly compromised. Our brains do not work well when we do not feel safe. When safety is uncertain, it becomes the mind's primary focus; when we feel unsafe, our first priority is to become safe again. Other matters that are usually of interest will become unimportant. For example, a toddler may be actively engaged in watching the family cat play with a ball. The toddler's excitement and focus are evident in his face, voice, and alert readiness to move. But then the cat decides to play with the toddler and scratches him. The sudden pain immediately leads to crying and searching for his mother or father, an attachment figure who will make the pain go away and in so doing restore his safety. We might confidently assume that such incidents represent the primary reason that attachment behaviors exist at all; they serve to ensure that a child is safe and to reestablish safety whenever the child is threatened.

In a related example, while watching the cat, the child hears his mother make a loud, unusual sound, and he immediately looks for his mother. If he sees her, he focuses on her face and movements to determine if she is safe or not, or if she thinks that he is safe or not. If he does not see her, he becomes anxious and waits expectantly for the next sign of what is happening. He might cry or scream, trying to elicit a response from her so that he can determine if he has reason to fear. During this entire sequence, the playing cat does not exist in his awareness. Enjoying or learning about cat play is of no concern until he has established that he and his mother are safe. If his mother is not safe, it is very likely that he is not safe either.

Establishing and maintaining a sense of being safe (along with actual safety itself) is the primary function of attachment figures for children. Once safety is created, the child is free to explore and develop fully based on his interests and capacities. However, safety cannot be taken for granted. It needs to be reestablished repeatedly for the child in response to his perceptions of threats. As he matures, he can be increasingly responsible for maintaining his own safety. However, during his early years especially, but also throughout childhood and adolescence and even into adulthood, his attachment figures are central in creating his sense of being safe.

Developing a Sense of Safety

The following ideas represent key features in ensuring a felt sense of safety for a child. This, in turn, is central to his ongoing well-being and development.

Ensure the Habitual Presence of an Attachment Figure

The felt sense of safety is maintained when preschool children are cared for consistently by one of a few secondary attachment figures whenever their primary attachment figure is not available. When such children are without any attachment figures, they tend to experience pervasive anxiety that may elicit intense, impulsive outbursts of distress or withdrawal into a passive state without expression of any affect, though intense emotion may exist internally. When day care provides such a secondary attachment figure, the young child tends to be able to adapt to the absence of the primary attachment figure with fairly brief distress that is relatively easy to regulate and integrate. Such secondary figures could be a relative or a day care provider in a homelike setting who gives ongoing attuned, individualized care. When day care is provided by adults who are only in the child's life for a few months because they are interested in other employment, or who are responsible for many children and do not get to know what is unique about each child, they do not become secondary attachment figures and do not provide the child with a sense of psychological safety even if they provide physical safety. This factor is very important when the child is under 3 years of age since a young child is less able to retain a sense of the permanency of attachment figures. These young children need one of their few attachment figures to be almost continuously present when they are awake if they are to be able to maintain a sense of safety and thus to be open to fully engaging in—and learning from—their environment.

Maintain Predictability

Predictability, with structure, routines, and rituals, creates a general sense of safety for a child. Within a stable—but not rigid—structure, variations in the primary features of daily life are minor, understood, and easily integrated. Providing many choices and free time certainly can generate an ability to develop interests, enthusiasm, and self-initiatives that may facilitate independence and creativity. However, such freedom may also generate anxiety and reduce safety when it does not match a child's readiness for such self-driven choices and behaviors—a readiness that may reflect his developmental age, temperament, confidence in a given situation, and general emotional and physical state at the time. The parent needs to find the balance between structure and flexibility, and she does so best when she is attuned to her child's response to structure and flexibility. She needs to remember that because her child responded to a given amount of free time yesterday does not mean that he will respond to the same amount today. Being attuned with the child—that is, being influenced intersubjectively—needs to be a routine habit for the parent if her decisions for her child are likely to be the most appropriate for him.

Enhance Safety When Disciplining

Discipline often consists of two features: an increase in safety and an increase in anxiety. Safety is enhanced though a child's knowledge that the parent is actively involved in a situation and has the knowledge and experience to best manage it. Anxiety is increased when the parent's decision about managing the situation is at odds with the child's wishes and thus may create frustration and conflict. Such conflicts may generate uncertainty about the meaning of the parent-child relationship, especially when the child is unclear about the parent's motives. To enhance perceived safety, the parent is wise to remember the probable value of the following:

- The parent should convey her decision regarding discipline within an open and confident stance, with clarity and information regarding her motives and the desired consequences. The intent of her communication is not to elicit agreement but rather to give the child the information that he needs to make sense of her decision. A focus on gaining the child's agreement may well communicate a fear of differences and conflicts and generate more confusion and less clarity for the child.
- The parent should be open to her child's perspective, so that he knows that she has confidence in her choice regarding what is best, while still knowing her child's wishes.
- The parent is wise to convey her decision with empathy for the frustration likely to occur due to the conflict between what the child wants and her decision. This will enable the child to experience understanding and comfort over his distress regarding the discipline, and to accept her decision more easily.

Plan in Advance for Changes and Separations

Significant changes, such as a move or a change of day care, need advance planning with the child being involved in the process. He needs information about what is happening, as he may interpret it as being caused by something negative about him. When he has some control over how it will happen, and when he is given an opportunity to meet new people and see his new home and community, he will have fewer fears and more opportunity to express them. He is also likely to benefit from participating in the process (e.g., decorating his new bedroom, showing his new day care provider something that is important to him).

When separations occur, due to regular events such as school, business trips, parental holidays, or overnights at a friend's house, as well as unusual events such as illness, moves, or death, it is wise to be aware that these may represent threats to a child's sense of safety. Separations are best dealt with by giving the child information about what is happening and how that is likely to impact his daily life. He will benefit from knowing where he will be, who he will be with, what he will be doing, and how long he will be separated from his parents. He also might be told what he and the adults who will be caring for him will do if he is upset or has a specific problem. Visiting the place where he will be and meeting his caregiver in advance is likely to increase his sense of safety. He should be given the opportunity to express any questions, fears, and opposition to the planned separation. Talking him out of his anxiety or talking over him with reassurance are only likely to increase his anxiety and resistance. He needs to be allowed to experience and accept his distress, even if it might cause his parents their own distress. He needs to be sure that his fears are understood before the parents' confidence that he can manage the situation will take hold. The parents also need to acknowledge, accept, and have empathy for his desire to avoid the situation. They need to accept his statement that he does not want the separation to occur and that it will be distressful to him, while at the same time conveying confidence that he (with the support of others) will be able to manage what he believes will be a difficult time.

Parents may also help their children with separations by providing them with concrete objects that will represent their continuing relationship (photos, articles of clothing, mementos, notes). The child might also be asked to give his parent something of his that the parent may keep with her throughout the day (thus reassuring the child that the parent will not forget him). Separations are discussed further in Chapter 9.

Avoid Isolation

Isolation as a response to anger may often be frightening to a child and may only intensify his anger. When he protests the act of discipline, or when discipline is required because of his behaviors, it is wise not to choose isolation as an additional consequence. When his emotions become intense, it is best to remain close to him so that he can rely on his parents' ability to regulate their own emotions, so that he can better regulate his own. Parents know this intuitively when their child is frightened or sad. The same applies when a child is angry. "Time-in" may well be a better alternative than "time-out" when time-out involves isolation.

Time-out may have value when the parent herself is dysregulated and so is not a source of safety for her child. Increasing dysregulation is likely to generate an escalation. At such a time, the parent needs a time-out more than the child does. When such separation is necessary, it is helpful for the parent to be clear that she is not rejecting her child. Saying something similar to the following might be more helpful:

> Hey, Jim, I am still worked up about what just happened between the two of us. I need to go into the family room for a bit to relax. We can talk later when we're both calmer.

If the child needs a short period of time alone to help him calm down, he should have the choice of separating himself from his parent, rather than it being forced upon him.

Be Deliberate With Surprises

Surprises need to be managed in a mindful manner. Prior thought is needed as to how the child is likely to experience a surprise, what he is losing by a change in the routine, and whether it is appropriate for his age. When recent, unexpected events have been stressful or traumatic (illness, an accident, death, divorce) then the child's first response to a surprise may be dysregulation and distress. Such a child may long for the safety of repetitive activities.

Surprises and excitement are not necessarily a positive experience for a child. They need to be compatible with his past experiences and expectations, and any anxiety associated with them needs to be adequately regulated. The parent needs to assess whether or not such surprises will be positive, based on her attuned sensitivity to her unique child and the situation.

Repairing the Sense of Safety

Daily life, for all of us and especially for children, often presents circumstances that reduce one's sense of safety. A conflict, an unpredictable event, or something that reminds us of a distressing experience in the past, can all produce a sudden change in our perceived sense of safety and leave us anxious and uncertain. Such events remain minor when they are recognized, addressed, and resolved either through reflective thought or through communication with another, especially an attachment figure. For children, the presence of an attachment figure who will assist the child in repairing the sense of safety is often crucial. As the child grows older, his own reflective abilities will enable him to often restore his sense of safety alone.

Relationship Repair

When there is a conflict between the parent and child that causes a break in the relationship, safety is enhanced when the parent actively facilitates a repair of the break as soon as possible. To maintain a sense of safety, the parent should not use "relationship withdrawal," meaning a refusal to talk to the child for an extended period of time as a consequence of his behavior. Such withdrawal generates fear of separation or even abandonment, which is likely to undermine a child's sense of safety. Relationship repair is discussed in much more detail in Chapter 9.

Be Sympathetic to Fears

When a child expresses irrational fears, it is important to remember that reason is often inadequate for managing fears, which is true for adults as well as children. If a parent begins to lecture a child, often with frustration and impatience, in response to her child's fears, the fears are likely to become worse. At those times the child is likely to sense that the parent does not understand and is not psychologically available to help the child manage the fear. When the child does not respond to the parent's rational approach to the fears, he is left feeling more hopeless since he is now failing in using the solution offered by his parent. The child now anticipates that he is likely to be alone— at least psychologically—when facing his fear. In contrast, when he has confidence that his fear is being taken seriously, when he senses his parent's empathy and understanding, he is likely to be much more able and willing to accept his parent's help and also to openly reflect on ways to manage the situation and reduce the fear.

Bringing Vague Fears Into a Dialogue

At times, a child will demonstrate a general sense of anxiety without being able to understand and describe the source of the anxiety. The child may be afraid to tell the parents about his fear, or the child may have no idea why he is afraid. Serious questioning of the child, focusing on potential problems and fears with a stern, and possibly equally anxious, parental attitude is likely to generate either no results or even greater anxiety within the child. A much more fruitful discussion would involve a meandering dialogue, conveyed in a relaxed, storytelling manner, about various events in the lives of the family members. Such a dialogue often enables the child to feel safe, which in turn is likely to make the child more ready and able to become aware of and then speak about events that are generating the anxiety. The development of such communication abilities is discussed in more detail in Chapter 6.

Obstacles to Maintaining a Sense of Safety

At times a single event (a trauma) or an ongoing situation (marital problems) may present a child with a much more difficult situation to repair. Such obstacles to re-establishing a sense of safety may require that the parent hold her child's distress in mind for a much longer period of time. The child may need to explore his fears a number of times in a number of situations. While they may appear to be resolved, they may unexpectedly re-emerge at a later date or under different circumstances. The parent's acceptance of the need for patience and re-exploring the distress a number of times with her child may be crucial to achieve an eventually full resolution of the impact of the event on the child.

Trauma

When a child experiences an acute, intense fear (such as being chased or bitten by a dog) or pain (such as surgery or a serious disease), or abuse (either by someone known to the child or a stranger), his sense of safety is greatly impaired and he is at risk to develop a traumatic response, which may create associated psychological problems. Attachment security, whereby the child is able to achieve a sense of safety or manage the fear or pain much better, serves as the best protection against the development of a traumatic response as well as encouraging the quickest resolution of any traumatic response that does develop. When faced alone, without the presence of an attachment figure on whom the child is able to rely, intense distress presents a much more serious problem to a child. It is crucial for the child to experience both his parent's support in managing the trauma and also his parent's confidence that he will be able to do so—with her help. If he experiences any parental fears that "he will never be the same," he will actually be at greater risk to "never be the same." If his parents have confidence that he will recover, he is more likely to do so.

Following an incident of acute fear, the child will be experiencing intense affective and physical dysregulation with possible crying, screaming, shaking, and repetitive movements and expressions. At that time, it is very helpful for his parent to accept and stay with him in his strong affective and physical state rather than trying to talk him out of it through quick reassurance, urging him to calm down, or trying to shock him out of it. Being with him, with congruent, animated affective and physical matching of his state is likely to provide him with the safety needed to confidently give expression in his emotion and body to the terror that he has just experienced. This will enable him to gradually release the terror through his movements and expressions. This general process whereby the parent is able to "coregulate" the child's dysregulated state is discussed further in Chapter 8.

After the parent has assisted the child to release some of the terror, she is in a position to assist him to reflect on the event in order to make sense of it to the degree that is possible. At that time, he is likely to be very receptive to his parent's reflective stance as well. Once the child has achieved some affective and physical mastery of his experience, he can begin to develop cognitive mastery as well.

Now, the child is ready to begin to reenter his daily life. Predictable routines that provide him with security and comfort will be especially important. Remaining close to his primary attachment figures is crucial to provide a sense of safety as well as for them to assist him by knowing when to introduce more of his daily responsibilities. The parent needs to be flexible about when her child is ready to return to school and other out-of-home experiences. She needs to convey confidence that he has the resources to face his daily challenges and responsibilities, while also communicating the need to be patient with the process and accepting the possible value of taking it slowly.

It may be that the acute experience of terror cannot be resolved without professional assistance. Trauma-focused therapies have been developed over the past 10 to 15 years that are quite effective in assisting adults and children to resolve single-incident traumas. These treatments are likely to be more effective with children who are securely attached to their parents. I also believe that parents should participate with the child in his treatment, but only if they are able to remain regulated during the treatment and be psychologically present for him. It is also likely to be helpful for the parents to meet with the therapist alone for a few sessions to explore ways that they might be more beneficial to their child's efforts to resolve the experience.

Marital Problems

Safety is threatened when there is marital discord or alienation that is either acute or chronic. Many factors are involved in such situations:

- Tension creates a family atmosphere whereby no one feels safe.
- Relaxed conversation and acts of sharing and altruism become infrequent and are overshadowed by conflict and emotional distance.
- Doubt is created regarding the future of the marriage and, necessarily, the future of the family. Financial security, moves and losses, and effects on parent-child relationships all become uncertain. The child may well imagine the possibility that one parent will disappear.
- Doubt is created regarding the child's role in causing the marital problems. With persistent doubt, shame is likely to follow.
- Anxiety is generated when the child feels responsible for helping his parents with their anxiety or depression regarding the problems.
- Anxiety is generated when the child feels responsible for being the peace maker and for preventing problems from occurring.

When marriage problems exist, the impact on the child's safety can be reduced by stating (with whatever words are clear to the child) what is already obvious to the child: "Marriage problems exist." This is best done by not providing details about the problems nor making promises about the future. When it is stated in a matter-of-fact manner, the child is left with the feeling that his parents are managing the situation and that, no matter what happens, they will be able to provide for their child's overall needs. The following remarks might help the child to feel as safe as possible within a situation that may cause distress, but can be managed and need not be traumatic:

> I'm sure that you've noticed lately that your mom [dad] and I have not been getting along that well. We have been

arguing more, and laughing and talking less, and just do not agree on things like we used to. None of this your fault, nor is there anything that you can do to help us with this. It is our job to work out these problems, not yours. And while we are working out the problems we will keep taking care of you. If you think that we are not caring for you the way we have been, please let us know. If you have questions about what is happening, please ask and we will tell you if we can. We both still love you so much, and that will never change.

Such a statement, while helpful, may not be sufficient if the child is thinking about the possibility of divorce. If that worry is evident, the parent might add, as long as it is true:

We aren't thinking about divorce at this time. We hope to avoid that and both of us are working hard to prevent it. However, if we don't succeed and do decide to get a divorce in the future, we will tell you about it in advance. It will not be your fault in any way, and we will both continue to love and take care of you. We will tell you how that will affect us all and how we will be caring for you.

Attachment-Focused Dialogue

The following example reflects a dialogue between a parent and child when the child is experiencing pain, with his sense of safety being jeopardized. The parent's response is based on the intention to facilitate her child's sense of safety before considering possible ways to manage the situation more easily. Ben is 7 years of age. He crashed his bike into a tree and landed awkwardly, breaking his leg, while also experiencing cuts and scrapes on his face and arms. He is being treated at an emergency room.

In this example, Ben's mother first communicates acceptance, understanding, and empathy for his anxiety and experience of pain. She does this by matching his voice rhythm, intensity, and pitch, as well as his facial expressions and possibly his gestures. His voice, face, and gestures are his nonverbal, affective expressions of his underlying emotion of fear and his experience of pain. By matching his affect, she is not communicating fear, but rather empathy; she is being with him in his fear. He experiences her empathy by perceiving her matched affective expression of his emotion. (There is a clear difference nonverbally between affect which represents the expression of one's own emotion, and affect which represents empathy for another's emotion.) Ben will not be confused by her matching his voice, face, and gestures. He will know that her affect represents understanding and empathy and he will feel safer, knowing that she is not frightened as he is.

Ben: Mom, it hurts so bad! Oh, Mom!!

Mom: I can see, Ben! I know it must hurt really badly! (Her arm is around his shoulder and she rocks with him in a soothing motion.)

Ben: It does mom, it really does!

Mom: Yes, Ben! I know sweetie, I know. And I'm going to stay with you the whole time you're here. I'll be right with you, Ben. (She strokes his hair and holds his hand while still rocking together.)

Ben: Make it stop, Mom! Make it stop!

Mom: Oh, honey, I wish I could. I truly wish I could.

Ben: Please mom, make it stop.

Mom: I can't, sweetie. I can't make it stop. But I'll be with you. I'll be right with you and at some point it will start to feel better.

Ben: When, Mom? When will it?

Mom: I don't know, honey. First the doctor will look at it and she'll let us know how long it will be.

Ben: But she'll make it hurt more! Don't let her, Mom. Don't let her!

Mom: Oh, sweetie, how scary that must seem to have the doctor look at your leg! I know, sweetie, I know it's scary! I'll be right with you!

Ben: Don't let her, Mom!

Mom: The doctor needs to see you, Ben. She needs to decide how to fix your leg. I can't do that, Ben. She needs to do that.

Ben: But it will hurt more, mom, if she touches it!

Mom: It might, for a little bit! But just for a short time, and then she will know how to make it better faster. She'll know, Ben, and then it will feel better, faster.

Ben: Mom, I want to go home! Can't we go home, Mom!

Mom: Oh, honey, I know how scary it is being here. I know, honey!

Ben: Let's go home now, mom! Let's go home!

Mom: We will honey, after the doctor fixes your leg and looks over the rest of those cuts you got. She needs to help you as much as she can. And then we'll go home, honey, then we'll go home. We'll go home together.

Ben: I want to go now, Mom!

Mom: I know you do, Ben. I know . . . I know . . . and I'll be with you the whole time we're here, honey. The whole time. I'm staying right here with you.

Ben: I'm scared, Mom! Please! (He is crying.)

Mom: Oh, sweetie! (Swaying back and forth as she strokes his hair, holds his head against her chest, and squeezes his hand tightly.) It must hurt . . . but you're safe now. You're safe with me. It will hurt some more, but I'll be with you. With me here, it will hurt less. It will hurt less.

Ben: Will it, Mom? Will it?

Mom: With me, honey, with me, it will be less. Yes it will. Yes, it will.

Ben: I love you, Mom. I love you.

Mom: And I love you, honey. You're my boy. You're my boy who I love so much. And we'll get through this together . . . yes we will.

CHAPTER THREE

Understand Intersubjectivity

Once safety has been established, an infant is ready to begin learning about the world. His learning comes from two primary sources: his body and his parents. His body is providing continuous input into his nervous system, whether it be from within—sensations of hunger, cold, sleepiness—or from the interplay between the child and the external world—touch, taste, smell, sounds, sights. The primary sensations of the external world that generate learning are those associated with his parents. His primary source of safety is also his primary source of learning. Starting while he is still in the womb, and for months and even years afterward, the primary source of his learning is his parents.

His first awareness involves his parents as being the source of his safety. When he is cold or hungry, his distress decreases when they touch him or introduce clothing or food. They respond to his negative physical and affective state and it goes away. When negative states dissipate, the young child begins to notice what is around him. He notices the colors, forms, movements, sounds, and varying pressures or movements against his skin. Within those sensations he tends to give priority to certain sounds (the high-pitched human voice) and certain forms (the human face). He prefers these objects to be active, and the activity that he most prefers is that which is responsive to his own activity. When he looks into the eyes of his mother, he is most interested when his mother looks back. When he hears his mother make sounds with her voice, he is most interested when her sounds are related in sequence, intensity, and rhythm to the sounds that he is making. Facial expressions that are similar to and respond to his facial expressions are those in which he has the greatest interest.

From the beginning, the activities of his parents that prove to be the greatest source of his learning are those which respond to and are contingent upon his own activity. This contingency—he initiates something and the mother responds, or she initiates something and he responds—provides him with a sense of agency, and of his own developing abilities to carry out his intentions. He can make changes in his world. He can influence his parents' behaviors to a great and satisfying degree, much more so than the behavior of the chair, lamp, apple, or even a mobile or cat. Along with a sense of agency, he begins to notice that his parents also initiate activity with him. They take the first step and when he responds, they respond to him. They introduce movements, sounds, and physical touches into his awareness, and then they respond to his response to them. Along with agency, the child is experiencing himself in a reciprocal relationship. Somehow his initiatives are connected to his mother's actions, and her initiatives elicit responses from him. This reciprocity, or this sequence of contingent responses, represents the onset of his communication with the world. Unique qualities of her responses are associated with unique qualities of his initiatives, and vice versa.

How and why is this important? These reciprocal interactions are the doorway into the child's learning. I am referring to social learning obviously, but also to emotional, psychological, communicative, cultural, behavioral, and even perceptual and physical learning. These reciprocal interactions represent how he begins to develop, deepen, and organize his experiences of his interactions with the world. What his parents are interested in influences what he is interested in. How his parents use their linguistic skills affects how he develops his own. The values and preferences of his parents naturally influence the development of his own. When his parents accept and respond to his initiatives, he tends to engage in those activities much more than those actions which his parents do not respond to, or respond to in a distressful way (an unpleasant voice or facial expression, or touch).

This reciprocal interaction affects the young child in an even more basic and crucial way in his psychological development. His parents' responses and interactions enable him to begin to develop a sense of self. Who he is, and who he discovers himself to be, is primarily the self that is seen, defined, and responded to by his parents. When his mother perceives him—making sense of his expressions and actions, as evidenced by the impact that they are having on her—he makes sense of his expressions in the same way. When his parents perceive him as being smart, he experiences himself as smart. Similarly, when they enjoy him, he experiences himself as enjoyable. When they are interested in him, take delight in him, and love him, he experiences himself as being interesting, delightful, and lovable.

Such communications become the template upon which the infant develops an experience of self. They profoundly impact the child's psychological development for better or for worse. Just as the child may conclude that he is enjoyable, he may also conclude that others do not enjoy him. He will think that he is boring if his parents are routinely bored with him. He will believe that he is deficient in some way or bad if his parents are habitually angry with him. He will conclude that he is unlovable if his parents routinely ignore him by failing to respond to him or initiate interactions with him.

During the first year of life, the infant becomes able to deduce his parents' intentions when they engage in nonverbal communications with him. When they point at a toy, he can understand that they want him to look at the toy. If they show delight when a song begins to play, he sees the effect of the song on them and, if they are looking at him, that they are suggesting that he may enjoy the music also.

At the same time, the infant is increasingly able to communicate his intentions to his parents. His behavior reflects his wish that they listen to a sound, get a toy for him, or play a game with him. When they respond to his wish, he is discovering both his ability to communicate and their desire to engage with him in the hoped-for manner. He can cause a response in his parents. He is empowered by having a positive impact on important others. The infant and parent are not simply imitating each other's behaviors; rather, they are engaged in a complex, nonverbal dance whereby they are both communicating their intentions, thoughts, and feelings, while also showing their interest in interacting with each other.

It is important to realize that this communication is entirely nonverbal and yet is extremely efficient and sophisticated. Parent and child are able to communicate their affective states, focus of attention, and intentional state easily and rapidly to each other. This communication is reciprocal and involves facial expressions, voice tones and rhythms, and gestures. Such nonverbal communication is thought to be ideal for engaging attention, communicating affect, and facilitating social interaction and language acquisition (Trevarthen & Aitken, 2001, p. 9).

Increasingly, the infant is able to learn about the world through observing the response of his parent to an object or event in the world. When a stranger enters or there is a loud noise, he looks at his parent's face to understand how his parent experiences that event. When he sees a new and interesting object, he shows it to his parents to see what they do with it. As he grows older, he carefully watches how his parents use tools, interact with neighbors, wash, and shave. He also closely observes what they take an interest in and what is not important to them. His developing interests, habits, and ways of interacting with others increasingly resemble those of his parents.

Intersubjectivity Throughout Childhood

Parents will recall such experiences with fondness. The look in a child's eyes and the expression on his face when he takes part in this intersubjective dance are not quickly forgotten by engaged parents.

We tend to forget that the infant's task of turning objects and events into experiences through his parents' experience of them is a neverending process. We tend to forget that, when it comes to emotional, social, and psychological realities, a child's life does not primarily involve learning about objective events. His life most often consists of converting these events and objects into subjective experiences, and the intersubjective matrix is the best context in which the organization and deepening of experience can occur. How objects and events affect significant others in our lives has a profound influence on how these objects and events affect us.

Intersubjectivity is about joining a child (or another adult) in his experience, experiencing it with him, matching his affective state, and exploring the experience with him to better make sense of it. It is simply that: being with another person in his experience. This is where the mind and heart meet. The inner worlds of both are creating an experience together. Even when a child is 10 or 15, how his parents experience him and his experience will deepen and change how he experiences himself and the world. This intersubjectivity will impact his behavior long into the future.

Since the adult's inner world has greater depth and breadth, by bringing her experience to the child's experience of an event, she is able to assist the child in regulating the affect associated with the experience and develop its meaning. When the child is securely attached to the adult, he trusts the adult with his inner life and is often eager to experience how the adult experiences his experience. It is less complex than it seems. When a young child sees his mother's eyes shine and her face express unlimited joy in response to his effort to put frosting on a cake, he experiences joy, pride, and satisfaction in a way that he never would if he were alone when he finished frosting the cake. That joint experience will influence how he finishes frosting the cake and how he approaches many such activities. If he sees sadness and disappointment in her face when he breaks his sister's toy, he feels remorse more acutely and can face what he has done more easily than if he was alone when he did it. When he is safe enough to experience her sadness over what he has done, he will be much less likely to do it again than if she had given him a severe consequence. His mother's intersubjective presence is all that he needs to manage the affect and learn deeply from both experiences.

If we focus on developing and maintaining intersubjective experiences with our children throughout their childhood, we will be able to better utilize these central experiences. These processes continue to exist within our emotional, cognitive, and neurological systems. If we simply are aware of them and take advantage of them, our child-rearing activity can be more spontaneous, natural, and effective. Our efforts to influence our child's development will have less need for lectures and consequences. The influence will just happen, often without any direct intention to make it happen.

The Three Features of Intersubjectivity

When parent and child are together, their experiences are not necessarily intersubjective. For an intersubjective experience to happen, there needs to be a matching of three central features of their inner lives. They need to share the same affective state, the same focus of awareness or attention, and the same intentions in the present moment.

The first quality, sharing an affective state, is known as *attunement*. When two individuals are attuned, they are in synch, so to speak, and manifest a similar degree of intensity in their present experience. This is evident in the rhythm of their expressions, with a matched degree of animation or peacefulness. I am not suggesting that they are matched emotionally (they need not both be happy or angry) but rather that they have the same quality of nonverbal expression. If one person is angry, the other is able to match the rhythm and intensity by which the anger is experienced and expressed without being angry herself. When this occurs, the person who is angry feels understood by the other. He knows that his parent gets it, in part because she tells him that she does with words, but primarily because she has matched his affective state.

Thus, when a child exclaims, "No one ever listens to me!" he will feel understood if his parent answers with the same rhythm and intensity, "No one! How hard that must be if it seems like no one listens to you!" If the parent had quietly said, "You think that no one listens to you when you talk," the child most likely would not feel understood. Rather, the child might feel more annoyed because such a quiet response might suggest that the parent didn't get it and was trying to manipulate the child to quiet down. With such a reply, the parent was not listening to the meaning of the nonverbal expression. The intensity and rhythm of the child's expression communicated how distressed he was and when it was matched, the child felt that the parent knew exactly how distressed he was. If the nonverbal expression is not matched, the child is likely to feel that the parent really did not understand the degree of his distress.

Matching the child's affect may seem to be harder than it is. As long as the parent's intention is to convey acceptance, understanding, and empathy for her child's emotion, the child will experience her affect as intended. If the parent's affect is expressing her own anger toward the child's behavior, the child will know that as well. If the parent's affect conveys sarcasm or criticism, the child will know that. The child will know the intention behind his parent's matching his affect. Such knowledge is not conscious but permeates our social awareness; infants are able to quite accurately begin to understand their parents' intentions toward them by the age of six months.

When a child is experiencing an intense emotion, the affective expression of it often has an agitated quality. When the parent matches the affect without having the same intense emotion, her affect appears to be animated. While she is calm inside, her matching affect shows a more rapid rhythm and greater intensity. The child's emotion leaves him dysregulated, causing an agitated affective expression. The parent's matching affect is animated, not agitated, because her emotions are remaining regulated. By so doing, the parent is helping her child's affect to become regulated again.

The second quality of intersubjectivity requires that the parent and child focus on the same object or event. If their attention is on different things, then they are not experiencing either thing intersubjectively. When they are sharing the same object or event together, such as a birthday card that the child received from his friend, they are experiencing it from different perspectives, and these shared perspectives influence the experience of each. In this example, the child may experience the card as not being that special, saying that his friend only sent the card because his mother made him. The parent might see the card as representing something very special about their relationship, and her belief, when openly shared, can readily change her son's experience. However, if she tries to convince him that her experience is right and his is wrong, the effect will be much less, if it happens at all. Intersubjective influence is much greater when it is simply an act of sharing experiences and not an effort to change the other's perception. Also, just as she can lead her child into sharing her positive experience of an event, she may lead him into sharing her negative experience of another event. His excitement may quickly decrease if she is distracted, not interested, or not impressed by something that he is telling her.

Because of the need for shared awareness, a parent-child dialogue that involves discipline often is not intersubjective. The parent wants both to attend to the same event (e.g., the child not taking care of his bike) whereas the child often is trying to be aware of something unrelated to the event. The parent then responds in frustration, "Pay attention to what I'm saying!" or "Quit trying to distract me!" By not sharing the same focus of attention, the child is trying to minimize the impact of the parent's apparently negative experience of the child at that moment. If she wants his attention, she is likely to have more success if she suspends all judgment about his motives while dealing only with his behavior.

The third component of intersubjectivity is shared, complementary intentions regarding their activity together. Frequently these shared intentions are to get to know each other, enjoy each other, communicate interest in a shared object or event, teach or learn about a shared interest, and give expression to the experience of one or both. When their intentions are different, the experience quickly loses its intersubjective quality. This happens when one wants to teach and the other does not want to learn, or vice versa. One wants to share an experience and the other does not want to understand. One wants to enjoy being with the other while the other would rather not be so engaged at that moment.

When we think about the three components of intersubjective experience, we can appreciate how central intersubjectivity is in human development. Shared affect, or attunement, can be seen as central in developing affect regulation abilities. Shared attention is central in developing the ability to expand one's attention span. Initially, the young child's attention rests upon his parent's much more extensive attention span, and his attention span stretches accordingly. Shared intentions are also central in the development of cooperation.

Examples of Intersubjective Development and Influence

Many events in a child's life introduce something new, unknown, confusing, or stressful. In order for the child to manage any emotions associated with that event and make sense of it, he will often benefit from joining with his parent's experience of that event. If she is managing her emotions and showing that she understands the event, the child will be much better able to manage his own emotions and begin to understand it as well. He is relying on her experience of such events in order to organize his experience of it. Sometimes the parent anticipates that her child will struggle with an event and she conveys her manner of dealing with it first. At other times she notices that her child is struggling with an event, so she joins him in his struggle, and shows him how to manage it.

Coping With Frustration

A 4-year-old shows frustration in his face while he tries to make his toy work. He suddenly screams and throws the car down, rests his elbows on his knees and his head in his hands, with evidence of his unhappiness on his face as he yells: "Stupid car!"

The child is taking the lead in communicating his strong experience of his inability to make the car work. When the parent responds in a contingent manner, she is making the experience intersubjective, which enables her to join him in his experience and assist him in organizing it. Thus she might say, with a voice tone similar to his in rhythm and intensity: "That's so hard when you can't make it work! So hard!"

She is matching his affective state, focusing on the car just as he is and showing her intention to understand and support him in his experience, and he is responding positively to her intention. She is communicating an understanding of the reason for his frustration, why it is so difficult, and even how difficult it is for him. Her response can enable him to communicate further about the experience: "I never can!" Her response might show an understanding that it might be harder than she first thought it to be: "Oh, my! You think that you *never* can do it! No wonder you are upset about it—if you *never* can make it work!"

Not arguing with her child, the parent has nevertheless helped the child to become aware that his distress relates to his immediate belief that he always fails to get his toys to work. Her ability to experience his discouragement is likely to help him reflect a bit and recall that at other times he was able to get it to work. He is then likely to grab the car again and maybe even carry it to his mother for help to make it work.

In this example, the parent simply conveyed her experience of her child's distress in a manner that enabled him to manage the emotion, reflect on the experience (with her awareness of its deeper significance for self), and continue with his original intention to fix the car. She assisted him in experiencing his frustration more fully, organizing it more deeply and broadly so that he was then able to approach the event more successfully. He did so because his mother was able to join him within the frustration, experiencing it with him and using her abilities to regulate affect and reflect on the situation to enable him to better develop his own experience.

Joining the Experience to Help Organize It

The intense stimulation and immediacy of an event are often too much for the organizational skills of a child's mind. Emotion may become dysregulated, resulting in the child's inability to attend to the event and maintain his original intention. Therefore the event might affect the child in this manner:

- Intense emotion, which is difficult to regulate (agitation, numbing)
- Intense avoidance, causing inattentiveness and distractions
- Lack of purpose, causing drifting or reactive impulsivity

When the parent joins the child's experience with her own (and her coherent sense of self with its ability to regulate and integrate experiences into her history), the following is likely to occur:

- Emotion is coregulated by the parent, reducing the intensity of the emotion.
- With regulated emotion, the child is able to attend to the event (while symbolically peeking at it from behind his mother's body).
- With renewed purpose, the child can respond to the event in a flexible way that is in his best interest, with the new meanings cocreated with his mother.

The child's experience of stressful events may generate shame, a sense of failure, or fear. The parent's different experience of those events can influence the child's experience of them. This would apply to a child's experience of a conflict with a friend, a trauma, loss, or failure to achieve a goal. It is more effective for the parent to simply present her experience as another way of experiencing the event than to argue that her way is right and the child's way is wrong.

Here are some other examples of a contingent—and most likely intersubjective—parental response:

- You really seem to be sad that I won't let you visit your friend.
- You look SO sad.
- You seem to be raring to go!
- You look kind of confused.
- You really look excited about getting it right!
- You seem to be so proud of what you just did!
- You really sound angry now!
- How hard that seems to be for you!
- You look relieved to be finished after all the work that it took.
- You really seem happy with your choice.

In these examples, the parent is following the child's nonverbal and verbal expression of his experience, joining him in the experience with matched affect and attention as well as complementary intentions. In so doing she is helping him to organize the experience and find words to describe it. Having words will help him to better manage similar experiences in the future.

The parent's nonverbal and verbal expression leads the child into giving further expression to his experience than he would do without his parent's active presence. Thus, reciprocal expressions such as these are likely to occur:

Parent: You really seem to be sad that I won't let you visit your friend now.
Child: I really want to see him!
Parent: Yes, you do! You really do.
Child: He's my friend and I miss him!
Parent: Yes he is! He's your friend. You miss your friend now, so much! Here, let me give you a hug. [Child seeks an embrace]

Parent: You seem to be so proud about what you just did!
Child: I did it! I can do it!
Parent: Yes! You're learning to do your puzzles.
Child: I'm learning to be a big boy!
Parent: Yes! You're learning so much. So much!

Parent: You really sound angry now.
Child: You won't let me watch tv!
Parent: Ah, that's why you're angry!
Child: I don't think you're fair!
Parent: So you don't think that I'm being fair to you!
Child: You're not! I don't like you!
Parent: So you're angry at me! I thought so!
Child: Yeah! You won't let me watch TV!
Parent: That's why! I thought that was the reason. And you don't like me now! I understand.

When a parent responds to a child's affective state (regardless of age) with similar vitality affect (nonverbal expression of intensity and rhythm) the child feels closer to the parent and the parent's experience of his own experience. Such natural responses are a core aspect of the child's sense that his parents understand him and that they can feel what he feels. When parents move into the more rational, teaching, lecturing mode as the child matures, they are decreasing their ability to influence their child through shared experience and to assist him in deepening and organizing his experience. They may elicit compliance and even passive agreement, but they are achieving their goal without actively involving their child in the process. His sense of self-efficacy and awareness of and confidence in his own inner life will be less. He might be able to manage his behavior reasonably well, until an event occurs that requires him to have the inner organizing skills necessary to choose the best possible behavior in a novel and stressful situation.

Leading the Child Into the Experience

In the above examples the focus was mostly on how the parent matches the child's experience. At other times, it is helpful for the parent to take the lead in communicating an experience that the child may not be experiencing himself. This does not necessarily mean that the child will experience the event as the parent did. The parent is not brainwashing the child. Rather, the child is simply exposed to the parent's experience, which might activate a similar latent experience within him. He is free to be influenced by his parent's experience of him or not.

For example, a parent may see her child through the window defending his friend against the teasing of another child in the neighborhood. Knowing that her child tends to avoid conflicts and seeing that the other child is bigger and somewhat aggressive, the parent is aware of how difficult it was for him to confront the other child. Shortly afterward, when he comes inside, she calls him over and says, with her hand resting on his shoulder: "That took such courage! I admire what you just did for Jake. I think that you really were a true friend for him when Ron was teasing him."

Her son quietly replies, "He would have helped me too."

Mom adds, "I know, you two are really good friends. And I also feel really proud about what you did right then. I think you were so brave!"

In this example, the child may not have shown nonverbally a sense of pride or an awareness of courage or being a true friend. He may have mostly been experiencing anxiety over confronting the older boy. When his mother experienced his courage and friendship, and her pride in him, he may have suddenly experienced himself with those characteristics for the first time during this event. His parent's experience of him helped him to organize his own experience of himself to include those traits. She led him into that experience rather than simply matching an experience that he already had. She invited him to experience himself similarly to how she was experiencing him. She did not force him to do so.

Other examples:

- Yes, I think you got it! I think you did it!
- Wow! I am amazed at what you just did!
- I think that is so wonderful!
- I'm really glad that you were able to be honest about that.
- I feel sad that you have to wait another day when it's so important to you.
- I'm really glad that you're happy with your choice.

For the child's impact on the parent to be experienced intersubjectively, it is very helpful for the parent to express the impact nonverbally, very explicitly and with emphasis. This nonverbal context for the words enables the child to experience them as being authentic and deep. Words alone may have a more shallow impact. The child may even think that the parent just said it because she had to as his parent and did not really mean them.

When the parent shows a strong response, she still needs to be very receptive to the child's response to her expression. The child may not be comfortable with her experience of him due to ambivalence about what he did or because his mother experienced his motives as being more positive than he did. He may then feel that he is fake and he has to hide his conviction that he really did not have the trait that she experienced (i.e., courage). He may experience himself as being deceptive and feel shame, which could lead to anger at his parent's positive expression. Thus, if the child challenges the parent's experience of him, that is not the time to argue. There is no right experience. If his experience of himself differs, it is best for the parent to adopt the same open, curious stance described above. While he may set aside his parent's experience, it is likely to remain in his memory and he is more likely to be receptive to—and notice—similar experiences (i.e., courage) in the future. Thus, in the above example when the mother described her experience of her son as being brave, he might have replied: "I wasn't brave! I was really scared. I didn't know what else to do."

Mom might then have replied: "Ah, you felt scared, not brave! So you want me know that."

> *Boy*: "Yeah, Mom, there was nothing to be proud of!"
> *Mom*: "I thought you looked kind of scared. So the feeling you had was scared! And you still helped your friend. Maybe the feeling was scared . . . and what you did was brave. Real brave, because you were real scared!

Another Example

Hank, 12 years old, had a conflict with some of his peers at school. Later he was discussing his experience of the event at home with his father. His father has a different experience about what the event means with regard to who Hank is. He then communicates his experience to Hank which, hopefully, will influence his sense of self.

> *Hank*: I never should have been there!
> *Dad*: What are you saying, Hank?
> *Hank*: I'm saying that maybe I deserved to have them make fun of me. Maybe I'm just the creep that they said!
> *Dad*: Wait a second now! Those kids laughed at you, which led you to yell at them, which led to a fight. So you think maybe you were responsible because the things that they said about you were true!
> *Hank*: That's it, Dad! Maybe I just need to face the fact that I don't have it!
> *Dad*: Hank, I'm sad that that's how you see it! That makes the whole thing that much worse, I would think. That somehow you're to blame—and you're to blame because now you are starting to see yourself they way they saw you.
> *Hank*: I don't know, Dad. Maybe they're right!

Dad: I'm sorry that you see it that way. That makes the whole thing so much more difficult, and I would guess, harder to let go of. Now you're moving into thinking that there is something wrong with you!

Hank: I don't know, Dad.

Dad: I can see that, Hank. Really hard, really confusing for you. I think that you've had a good sense of who you are and now you have doubts.

Hank: I do have doubts.

Dad: I don't. I know who you are, but I don't think what I see about you is that clear to you now. You don't see in yourself what I see, right now.

Hank: What's that?

Dad: Someone who is honest, and has courage, and tries to do what is best for others, and is kind of hard on himself some-times. Eventually you will step back and see the person that I see! It's like that is all covered with fog for you.

Hank: Maybe you're right, Dad. When do you think the fog will go away?

Dad: I can't say for sure, but my love might help . . . and so might this hug . . . and so might your giving it some more thought, wondering a bit about who you are . . . really are, that those guys can't or don't want to see.

Repairing Intersubjectivity

Sometimes the child may not accept his parent's experience of what he is experiencing. The parent may express sadness in response to her sense that her child is sad, and the child may say with impatience, "I'm not sad!" At that point, it is important for the parent to respond by accepting the child's response, and possibly being curious about what he is experiencing if it is not sadness. To argue with a child about what he is experiencing suggests that the parent knows the child's inner life better than he does. Such a suggestion could undermine the child's confidence in himself and his readiness and ability to sense his own thoughts, perceptions, feelings, memories, and wishes. It could undermine his intuitive sense about what is best for him. It certainly is possible that the parent may be right, that the child actually does experience the event in that manner. If that is true, the parent's initial expression is likely to help the child be aware of it in the future or be open to the possibility that he had such experiences. But for the parent to insist that she is right will have negative effects on her child. Besides undermining his confidence in his own intuition about what is best, it is likely to create resistance and distance in the parent-child relationship. He is likely to experience it as an intrusion into his life and to communicate less about his experiences in the future in order to protect them from similar intrusions.

For example, John sees his daughter Sharon sitting in the living room after her mother told her that she could not go with her to the store.

John: You look sad.

Sharon: I'm not sad!

John: Oh, okay. You're sitting here by yourself, but not sad. What are you feeling?

Sharon: Nothing!

John: Okay, nothing. . . . The way you were sitting here made me think you were having a hard time!

Sharon: I'm not having a hard time!

John: I know that you wanted to go with your mother!

Sharon: So!

John: I thought you were disappointed when she was talking with you.

Sharon: I wasn't!

John: So it's hard to know . . . and I think that whatever is going on, you'd rather not talk with me about it.

Sharon: That's right!

John: You might be thinking, "Nothing Dad says is any help. I want to go with Mom!"

Sharon: Well, nothing will help.

John: That's right, Sharon. Nothing will help you to be able to go. . . . I was just hoping that I might help a bit with anything that might be going on now with you.

Sharon: You can't! Just leave me alone!

John: I will if you want. I'll be thinking about you in the other
    room if anything comes up.

Here, John was available, sensitive, and responsive to his daughter's
request that he not respond to her at that time. By accepting his
daughter's wish to be alone, after inviting her into a dialogue, John
was maintaining an intersubjective presence that most likely indi-
rectly helped his daughter to manage the experience better.

Parents are wise to provide at times—with empathy—a tentative
experience of their child's experience while at other times providing—
with curiosity—an open stance that tries to understand, without
judgment, what the child is experiencing that led to his behavior. Together, both convey an active interest in understanding the child's
inner life without "reading his mind." At times the parent initiates a
tentative, empathic focus on his inner life and at other times follows
with curiosity his reflecting on his inner life. Parent and child, together, are cocreating his experience of his inner life.

The parent's curiosity is nonjudgmental. It does not lead to questions whose motives are to catch the child in faulty thinking. Rather,
curiosity is motivated by her desire to understand her child better
and then to assist him in managing any strong feelings that he may be
having. She assists him in reflecting on his inner life, rather than changing it. Once his inner life is made clear—to both child and parent—her
attuned presence is more likely to be experienced as being motivated by her desire to help him manage a situation so that it is best
for him, rather than a desire to change him so that the situation is
best for her. He then experiences her subjective presence as being
aligned with his own. His subjective experience is important to her.
When his mother takes this open, nonjudgmental stance with her
child, he is likely to be much more receptive to her assistance.

This mother is assuming that her child is doing the best that he can
to achieve the result that will be best for him. She may believe that
his choice is in error because he is overlooking what is best for someone else or the more distant consequences of his actions, and she
may be correct. However, to help her child experience the impact of
his behavior on others or the consequences of his actions, she is going

to be more effective if he experiences her aid as coming from understanding and empathy, rather than from a stance that simply attempts to control his behavior.

Often we assume that we know how a child is experiencing an event when, in fact, we do not. We may assume that a child is annoyed when he is really frightened and is concealing his fear. We may assume that he is doing something to get our attention when he is really doing something because he wants to become more skillful at a task. We may assume that he knows that we set a limit to ensure that he will be safe, when he thinks that we set the limit to make him unhappy. When such assumptions are faulty—when we are not reading our child correctly—he will not feel understood nor think that we are empathizing with him. If we are wrong, our intervention may not only be unhelpful, it may make the situation worse. It is often better to delay making a judgment about a child's inner life. If a child is uncertain about his experience, we may help him by making guesses about it, not assumptions. It is better to have an open, curious stance about what factors within the child caused his behavior rather than believing that we know how he felt.

Another Obstacle to Intersubjectivity

For the intersubjective to be present, it needs to have an impact on both individuals who are experiencing it. The parent's impact on the child's developing experience is generally the greater of the two, but the child's experience still will have an impact on his parent's experience. This is evident when they share something that the child is proficient in, such as computers. It is especially true with regard to the parent's experience of herself as a parent.

When a parent sees her child experiencing joy, delight, enthusiasm, and confidence during their intersubjective time together, she most likely will know that she has contributed to her child's experience and will feel pride and satisfaction for her child, as well as pride and confidence in herself as a parent. These moments of deep sharing and her sense of how important they are for her child's development are among the most rewarding moments that a parent can have.

However, during other intersubjective experiences, the child may experience the parent as being mean, selfish, bossy, or uncaring. He may think her interests or values are wrong, irrelevant, or silly. Since the parent is open to being influenced by her child's experience—otherwise it would not be intersubjective—the parent might well be somewhat vulnerable to her child's negative experience of her and what is important to her. Sometimes parents deal with that difficulty by not allowing the child to express his negative experience. Sometimes parents deal with it by giving in to their child's wishes so that his experience of them will become positive. In the first example, a parent is denying her child the ability to influence her. In the latter example, a parent is giving up her ability to influence her child.

To maintain reciprocity, safety, and emotional intimacy in the face of a child's negative experience of his parent, it is helpful for the parent to try to understand her child's experience, rather than assuming that he has negative motives. If she is open and accepting of his negative experience of her, it is likely to decrease and the difference will have no effect on the inner self of either of them, nor on the relationship.

The following dialogue between Shawn and his mother helps illustrate this.

Shawn: I think that you're just being mean!
Mom: Oh, you think that's why I said no—I'm just a mean mom.
Shawn: Yeah! You are!
Mom: I'm sorry, Shawn, that you think that. That would make it hard to feel close to to me right now. Real hard!
Shawn: I don't want to be close to you!
Mom: That's what I thought. You seem to want to handle it all by yourself.
Shawn: I do. . . . Why can't I do it?
Mom: Shawn, I can see that you really want to.
Shawn: I do.
Mom: Here, I have an idea that might help.

She takes his arm and leads him to another thing that he might do. Within a minute he has forgotten his anger and his experience of his mother as mean, now likely replaced with her as being simply his mom.

Attachment-Focused Dialogue

Jenny, a 12-year-old girl, had been playing basketball for a number of months on the school team. She had taken up the sport a few years before and her skills were definitely improving. She made two great plays during the final minutes of a close game that helped her team win. However, in the car on the way home from the game, Jenny was surprisingly withdrawn. Her Dad decided to pull over and go for a walk in the park before returning home, where Jenny would have to face her brothers. As they started to walk, he commented on Jenny's great game.

Jenny: I got lucky! I'm really not that good.

Dad: My goodness, Jenny. I was so happy for you. You really helped to win the game. But you don't seem very pleased about it. What's that about?

Jenny: I got lucky! It will be a long time before I do that again.

Dad: So it seems to you that what you did is not much to be happy about?

Jenny: Why should I be? It won't happen again!

Dad: It seems to be really hard for you to see what I see. I don't mean that you will make great plays to win every game. I mean that I see you getting better and better almost every time you play.

Jenny: But I'm still not that good!

Dad: You really are hard on yourself today, Jenny. What do you think that's about?

Jenny: I just don't want everyone to think that I'm the best player on the team.

Dad: Ah. I think I understand better. You had a great game and you might be worrying that people will expect that every game.

Jenny: Yeah! I'm not the best one on the team. There's a lot of girls better than me.

Dad: So, Jenny, if we forget the other kids for now . . . do you think that you're a pretty good player and that you're a lot better than you were last year?

Jenny: I guess.

Dad: Oh, I'm glad, because that's how I see you! You've come so far, in really not very much time. And I would hope that you might be proud of yourself. A bit anyway. Not comparing you to the other kids on the team. Just to yourself, and how you were last year. I think that you're doing pretty darn well. Yes I do!

Jenny: Okay. I guess I'm doing pretty good.

Dad: Great! I'm so glad that you can enjoy what you've done— how far you've come—and feel some pride in yourself. You've worked hard to get this far.

Jenny: I guess.

Dad: You guess! You're put so much of yourself into it. Please enjoy it, a little bit anyway.

Jenny: I said, okay.

Dad: You didn't say you'd enjoy it.

Jenny: Okay! I'll enjoy it!

Dad: Great. We both will then. I am proud of you.

Jenny: I know, Dad.

Dad: And I don't expect you to win every game with a great play. And you don't have to be the best girl on the team for me to still be proud of you.

Jenny: I don't?

Dad: Oh, Jenny. I'll be proud of you if you hardly ever get into the games. I know that you try, that you enjoy basketball, that you're a good teammate. I'll always be proud of you and who you are, in everything you do.

Jenny: You have to . . . you're my Dad.

Dad: I'm your dad, yes . . . and I have to because I know you so well and I am amazed at the person you are becoming. Truly amazed. And it does not matter if you steal the ball or make the winning shot. I will always be amazed at the person you are and the person you are becoming.

Jenny: That's because you're . . .

Dad: Give it up! [They laugh together.] It's because of who you are!

CHAPTER FOUR

Recognize Your Own Attachment History

The importance of attachment security in the development of the child is, hopefully, evident by now. What might be less clear is how important the parents' own attachment histories are in determining whether their child will attain a secure attachment with them. This close connection between the parents' and child's attachment abilities is due to the nature of both psychological safety and intersubjectivity.

When a child turns to his parent for safety due to exposure to a perceived threat or to his own emerging dysregulating emotion, the parent needs to feel safe herself in the situation if she is to enable her child to feel safe. If the event—such as a loud noise or an approaching stranger—elicits fear in the parent, then the parent will not be a perceived source of safety for the child. Instead, the parent's fears are likely to make the child's fears even more acute. The parent needs to manage her own fears before she will be available to help her child manage his fears. Intersubjectively, the child is looking to the parent's experience of the event to determine his own experience. If the parent does not feel safe, how can the child expect to feel safe? Or if the child's strong emotional state—anger, fear, sadness, shame—tends to elicit a similar, dysregulating emotional state in the parent, then the parent's presence is likely to cause the child's emotion to be even more dysregulating, rather than less.

Intersubjective states are reciprocal. That is, the affect, awareness, and intention of one has an impact on the inner life of the other. We have seen how a calm emotional state in the parent can have a calming effect on a distressed child when she matches the child's affective expression of his emotion. On the other hand, the distressed state of the child may cause distress in the parent. An enraged state in the child may cause rage in the parent. In such cases, not only is the parent failing to facilitate a sense of safety within her child; she is actually causing the child more distress. He turns to his parent for safety and his parent's distress increases his own fears.

For attachment to become secure, the most important time for the parent to be available, sensitive, and responsive to the child is when the child's attachment needs are the most activated. A parent may be appropriately responsive most of the time, but her child still may be insecurely attached if she is not appropriately responsive during the most critical times. For that reason, the parent's own attachment history needs to be resolved.

Developing Autonomous Attachment

Attachment security in adulthood is known as *autonomous attachment*. This means that attachment security can be attained, while at the same time, the adult is able to function autonomously. She does not have to sacrifice her individuality to maintain attachment security with her partner and best friends. She also does not have to sacrifice her intimate relationships to achieve autonomous functioning.

It is not necessary for a parent to have experienced attachment security during her own childhood in order to be a secure attachment figure for her child. Of course, if she was securely attached during her childhood there is a good probability that she will be autonomously attached as an adult and that her child will also be securely attached to her. However, if she can attain attachment security as an adult, even though she was not securely attached to her parents when she was young, her child is still likely to become securely attached to her. The crucial factor is whether or not she has resolved the factors from her youth that prevented her from becoming securely attached then. It is her current attachment state of mind that affects her child's attachment.

An adult can resolve destabilizing aspects of her attachment history if she can reflect upon those events, regulate the affect associated with them, reexperience the events from a new perspective, and then integrate her new experience into her autobiographical narrative. This means that she can now recall any event from her past that relates to her attachment history without being pulled into the dysregulating affect of pervasive shame, rage, terror, or despair. There is no longer any aspect of her past that she needs to avoid or distort. She is able to make sense of, accept, and develop an awareness of how the event affected her history and self-concept, all while remaining fully aware of the present and the future.

For various reasons, childhood events may have not been resolved and may be very hard to remember as an adult. An event may have caused a clear trauma, such as something involving abuse, abandonment, loss, rejection, or ridicule. More than likely, that trauma did not become associated with protection, comfort, and support from the child's parents at the time. The active presence of a parent might well have enabled the child to integrate the trauma and so resolve it. However, more often unresolved events are not associated with a particular trauma, but rather involve the child's parents psychologically being critical, rejecting, or unavailable when the child was experiencing something stressful or uncomfortable. The child may have experienced routine anger, fear, sadness, or shame, and his parents may have rejected aspects of his response to that experience, preventing the child from integrating it into his history.

When the parent is able to resolve her history, she then can remain psychologically and physically present for her child when her child's attachment needs are activated. She is able to respond to her child's agitation with sufficient affect regulation to enable her child to achieve better affect regulation. She is coregulating her child's affective state.

She can also respond to her child's confusion and doubt about the situation with sufficient reflective abilities to enable her child to achieve another perspective regarding the event. Her child then is able to reflect on the event and integrate it into his life narrative. She is cocreating a new way to experience the event—to give the event a new meaning.

Reorganizing Attachment Patterns

When a parent realizes that her own attachment history is insecure and that she has not resolved important events in her history, she needs to know that she can address her unresolved experiences and work toward achieving autonomous attachment. Attachment patterns are stable, but they do not need to be rigid. They can change based on new relational or reflective experiences that facilitate their resolution. An adult who is able to develop and maintain an emotionally intimate relationship with a partner or best friend is often in the best position to resolve past events from her attachment history. An adult may also attain more secure attachment functioning through establishing an emotionally meaningful relationship with a therapist who is able to assist her in reexperiencing her past and its influence on her present and future.

Unresolved events from an adult's attachment history are those which, when they approach awareness now, tend to dysregulate her affective and reflective functioning so that she is not able to make sense of them and manage their dysregulating effects. The emerging memory elicits the overwhelming emotions and thoughts that occurred during the original event. If, when she was a child, her father screamed at her and threatened to send her away to a boarding school, the terror and shame that she felt then may be experienced in the present almost as strongly as they were originally. If in the past, the terror and shame caused her to avoid all interaction with her father, all situations and behaviors likely to cause a similar threat from him, or all feelings and wishes that led to her behavior, then she is likely to have similar reactions in the present when those memories are activated.

Possibly her father's angry threats were overwhelming to her because she was not able to turn to her mother to regulate her inner life and come to a resolution and relationship repair with her father. Or her father did not apologize and initiate relationship repair with her. If associated memories are activated in the present by her child's behavior, she is likely to experience similar terror and shame, or she may react with rage or despair in her position as an adult. In such situations, if she is able to turn to another adult who can serve as an attachment figure, she will be in a better position to regulate the emerging thoughts and feelings associated with the past event. If her partner or friend can help her regulate her reaction to her child's behavior, she will be able to maintain a regulated response to that behavior.

At these times, the parent benefits most from her partner's, friend's, or therapist's empathic presence and unconditional acceptance. She will benefit much less from problem solving, at least until she is able to regulate her inner life. Her partner's acceptance, curiosity, and empathy will enable her to feel greater self-acceptance, self-awareness, and self-empathy. She will then be able to reexperience the past event with more confidence that she has the strength to manage it in her mind and to make sense of it in ways that are less shameful and frightening. The presence of her attachment figure—her partner, friend, or therapist—enables her to remain aware of her inner life without dysregulating and to make sense of the past so that it no longer overwhelms her. In so doing, she is then much more able to remain present when her child is dysregulated.

A parent may also be able to facilitate the development of autonomous attachment through reflective functioning developed through meditation or similar mindfulness exercises (Siegel, 2007). By doing so she can achieve greater self-attunement, which improves self-acceptance, awareness, and empathy. She will have greater patience with herself and a lighter response to her own mistakes. She will be able to treat herself the same way that she might treat her child if he is to be securely attached to her. Combining such self-reflection and self-attunement with the attuned, intersubjective experiences of an emotionally intimate relationship is likely to be the most effective way to remain fully present for her child when his attachment needs are the most active.

Reflecting upon her attachment history can facilitate her ability to remain regulated when her child's behavior activates specific memories from her childhood. Questions suggested by Dan Siegel and Mary Hartzell (2003) serve as an excellent starting point for such self-reflection (Table 4.1). The more the parent can recall any aspect of her attachment history without experiencing dysregulating fear, shame, rage, or despair, the more she will be ready and able to assist her child when he is becoming dysregulated. No event from the past will require her mind to distort or deny its reality due to terror or shame. It is hard for a person to feel safe—either a child or an adult—when that person is afraid of his or her own mind. To be able to reflect on any memory or associated thought, feeling, perception, or wish without terror or shame can offer a vast sense of freedom.

Some parents may fear that such reflection or exploration with a significant other will cause a break in their relationships with their own parents. However, such a result seldom occurs because the intention of reflecting on the past is not to right the perceived wrongs of childhood. Rather, the intention is to make sense of the stresses, conflicts, unresolved issues, and avoided themes in the family in order to understand their impact on a person's development.

The intention is not to find someone to blame for past events that are difficult to address, but rather to simply begin to address them. That does not mean that an adult has to confront her parents or siblings. In fact, often when she is able to make sense of the past, she discovers that it is easier to let many of those events go. She is more likely to conclude that her parents did the best that they could, that they did not intend to hurt her and make her life more difficult, and that they may have, in fact, raised her better than they were raised themselves. However, she may conclude that she must separate from her parents psychologically in order to be able to begin to develop a sense of safety within herself and provide the same sense of safety to her children. Through reflecting on her attachment history, she is in the position to freely choose what course of action is now in her best interest.

TABLE 4.1 Questions for Parental Self-Reflection (Siegel & Hartzell, 2003)

1. What was it like growing up? Who was in your family?
2. How did you get along with your parents early in your childhood? How did the relationship evolve throughout your youth and up until the present time?
3. How did your relationships with your mother and father differ and how were they similar? Are there ways in which you try to be like or try not to be like each of your parents?
4. Did you feel rejected or threatened by your parents? Were there other experiences you had that felt overwhelming or traumatizing in your life, during childhood or beyond? Do any of these experiences still feel very much alive? Do they continue to influence your life?
5. How did your parents discipline you as a child? What impact did that have on your childhood and how do you feel it affects your role as a parent now?
6. Do you recall your earliest separations from your parents? What were they like? Did you ever have prolonged separations from your parents?
7. Did anyone significant in your life die during your childhood or later in your life? What was it like for you at the time, and how does that loss affect you now?
8. How did your parents communicate with you when you were happy and excited? Did they join with you in your enthusiasm? When you were distressed or unhappy as a child, what would happen? Did your father and mother respond differently to you during these emotional times? How?
9. Was there anyone else besides your parents in your childhood who took care of you? What was that relationship like for you? What happened to those individuals? What is it like for you when you let others take care of your child now?
10. If you had difficult times during your childhood, were there positive relationships in or outside your home that you could depend on during those times? How do you feel those connections benefited you then and how might they help you now?
11. How have your childhood experiences influenced your relationships with others as an adult? Do you find yourself trying not to behave in certain ways because of what happened to you as a child? Do you have patterns of behavior that you'd like to alter but have difficulty changing?
12. What impact do you think your childhood has had on your adult life in general, including the way in which you think of yourself and how you relate to your children? What would you like to change about the way you understand yourself and relate to others?

Establishing the ability to reflect on her childhood, the parent tends to become more flexible and aware in her responses to her own children. She discovers that she is less likely to react to them the same way her parents reacted to her (or did not react). Rather, she is more likely to perceive the child's inner world more openly and without judgment and will be more able to accept and even respond with some pride when her child's inner life is different from hers and he feels free enough to communicate these differences.

Obstacles to Reorganizing Attachment Patterns

High demands, responsibilities, and stress in the present can make it difficult to reorganize an insecure attachment in adulthood. When the parent has an unresolved attachment history and the child manifests closely related attachment difficulties, the stresses of daily family life often make it hard to step away from immediate situations and reflect on past events. When things are difficult, the appeal of a quick fix is considerable, and it is tempting to focus on behavioral techniques based on consequences. It takes confidence and trust to turn your gaze to the difficulties of the past when the difficulties of the present are so demanding. When looking at the past makes sense to the parent and she is committed to doing it, there is a good chance that she can find a way to manage the current situation so that it does not get worse, while placing much of her attention on her own history. She may solicit greater assistance from her partner, other family, and friends in the short term. She might also institute a more structured day, as well as the other suggestions found in Chapter 10, to reduce conflicts and distress. Such interventions need to be applied with PACE (see Chapter 5) if they are to have lasting benefits.

Another obstacle is a lack of attachment figures for safety and self-exploration. It is very hard to raise children and even more difficult when your history is unresolved and the child's behavioral difficulties are becoming more intense. Being able to rely on someone while exploring your own history is very beneficial and often necessary if resolution is to be achieved. Seeking therapeutic help may be necessary.

A third obstacle is very extensive and rigid unresolved attachment patterns. While often a parent's own attachment history contains sufficient areas of resolution and coherence to make the resolution of other areas not too difficult, at times the history is replete with childhood trauma, neglect, separations, and losses, rendering it very hard to begin to integrate and resolve the attachment history. In such cases, an extended course of therapy may be necessary.

Attachment-Focused Dialogue

In the following conversation, a mother had a particularly hard day with her 10-year-old daughter when they were home together most of the day while her husband and 8-year-old son were away from home. That evening when her children were in bed, she approached her husband out of concern over the conflicts between her and her daughter, which were not uncommon in their relationship.

Jen: I never felt so glad to see you and Dan come walking in the door. Kim and I just could not get along all day. [with a tired and discouraged expression]

Matt: What was going on? [interested, curious, and non-judgmental]

Jen: Oh, I don't know. I guess we were okay at first, but then something just got us going.

Matt: Any sense of what it was?

Jen: Yeah . . . now I know. I told her that if she would help me get the table cleared after breakfast, we would drive over to that new deli and I'd get her a decaf mocha that she likes and a latte for me. Just a nice little time to relax and chat before we got busy.

Matt: And . . .

Jen: She didn't help at all. Then she went and turned on the TV. So I cleaned up a bit and asked her if she wanted to go to the deli, hoping that might motivate her to help. And she said no.

Matt: She just wanted to hang around the house?

Jen: Maybe, but it seems that she is always on me for not doing things with her, for not being home, and now we had a

chance—just the two of us—and she wasn't at all interested. She didn't want to do anything with me.

Matt: And you were hoping for some nice, close time!

Jen: Yeah, what's wrong with that? I wasn't asking her to work
all morning. Just to spend a little time together. Maybe get
along for a change.

Matt: And it backfired.

Jen: It did! So I left the family room, finished clearing up the
table myself, and I was getting more upset by the minute . . .
and that TV was on loud, so I yelled for her to turn it down.
She didn't, so I yelled again, and she said that she had
turned it down, and I yelled, "Not enough," and nothing
happened so I went in and turned it down myself. So she
yelled, "That's great! Don't you have anything better to do?"
Of course I had to answer that and off we went.

Matt: I'm sorry, honey. It seemed like you really wanted to be
close to Kim and it did not work out. You ended up further
apart than when you started.

Jen: I get so tired . . . nothing I ever do seems to be good
enough for her. Nothing gets through to her. Nothing about
us matters to her.

Matt: You are discouraged.

Jen: Well, that's what it seems like sometimes . . . like she really does not want to be close to me. What have I done wrong?

Matt: You're really discouraged and hard on yourself.

Jen: Shouldn't I be? I would have given anything when I was
her age for my mother to offer to spend a morning with
me . . . just the two of us. She was always too busy for that.
Something else was always more important than me. So I
decided that when I had a child I would never treat her, or
him, the same way. I would make time. I would want to
spend time with my child. And now I do, and she does not
want to spend time with me!

Matt: So you're saying that it's the same as it was with your
mother?

Jen: Yes! My mother didn't want time with me. Kim doesn't
want time with me. First my mother rejects me and now my
daughter rejects me. I'm the one getting rejected both times.

Matt: So no matter how different you tried to be with Kim than your mother was with you, the results seem to be the same.

Jen: So again, I must be the one in the wrong. I'm doing something wrong again!

Matt: Again! You're blaming yourself for your mom not spending more time with you?

Jen: No, it couldn't have been me then . . . but it sure felt like it when I was Kim's age. It felt like I was just not a good enough daughter. If somehow I could be better, maybe my mom would like me more, want to be with me. I felt that for so long . . . until maybe I just didn't think about it much. Somehow I just accepted that was the way it was and I stopped trying to be close to her.

Matt: And now you think that Kim does not want to be close to you.

Jen: That's what terrifies me! Somehow I'm afraid that she will become with me like I am with my mom—polite and distant. Mom and I have our own lives, and don't share our lives with each other much. I fear that Kim and I will never be close. No matter what I do, I'll never be the mom that she would want to be close to.

Matt: Oh, sweetie, now I understand how hard today was for you. It seems to be a sign of you and Kim drifting apart. In a way, like you're losing your daughter.

Jen: I'm so scared of that! So scared! What can I do? What am I doing wrong?

Matt: Are you trying too hard?

Jen: What do you mean?

Matt: I don't know. It just seems to me that you're a wonderful person and Kim is a delightful girl. You both have so much going for yourselves. Maybe you're trying too hard. Maybe if you just let your love be there, be with her, maybe she would respond more easily. Just like you would have done if your mom had shown her love for you more clearly and easily.

Jen: But I want so much to make it happen!

Matt: You don't trust that it would happen on its own?

Jen: Maybe I don't have confidence in my love. Maybe . . . maybe it didn't work with my mother. No matter how much

I loved her, she still didn't find time for me. Maybe I don't trust just loving Kim . . . maybe I have to make her take it. Oh, I don't know. But maybe . . . maybe . . .

Matt: What are you saying, honey?

Jen: That maybe . . . I have to make her take my love because she is not likely to take it on her own. Why would she? My mom never did! [cries]

Matt: Oh, sweetie . . . this mother-daughter thing, you have so many doubts.

Jen: It's not that. No . . . it's what I'm doing with it!

Matt: What do you mean?

Jen: It's one thing to have doubts. Okay. I can manage that. But it's what my doubts are causing me to do with Kim. I'm giving her no choice. She has no say in this. I want to love her so she has to receive it. Or I get mad at her! She has no way to be her own person who sometimes just wants to be different. Who sometimes just wants to be alone, or be with her friends. Who wants the freedom to have a say in whether or not we share. And I haven't given her that free-dom. She has to accept my love or I get mad. I feel rejected and think, "How dare she!" Oh, my. Oh, Matt . . . I wanted Kim to meet my need to have her accept my love. I didn't want her to be her own person, because I was afraid . . . and still am, that if she is her own person she would choose not to love me in return.

Matt: You don't think that she would want from you what you wanted when you were her age?

Jen: My brain says that she would, but I don't have confi-dence in it. So I have to make it happen. In that way I've been trying too hard. To be my daughter, Kim has to give up herself! To be close to me . . . she can't be separate from me.

Matt: Wow! Do you think that's it?

Jen: It makes sense, Matt. It really does! I need to let her be herself. I need to let her be who she is and let our relation-ship become the way it becomes.

Matt: Do you know what I'm hearing?

Jen: What?

Matt: I'm hearing you talk about your love for Kim. No matter how hard it is for you. No matter how scared you get about not being close . . . for her you will take the risk . . . because you love her.

Jen: I have no choice—because I love her.

Matt: And she will know that. At some level she will know and she will choose to be close to you often. And not because you insist. Because she wants to.

Jen: I hope so, Matt. I hope so. But I will not sacrifice her to get it.

Matt: I know that, Jen. I know that. That's one of the many reasons I love you.

Jen: You do, don't you?

Matt: I do. And you don't really try hard to get me to love you. I do because of who you are.

Jen: And you make it so easy to love you, Matt . . . because of who you are.

This conversation between Jen and Matt could happen because Jen had achieved some resolution of her experience of her mother not being available for her emotionally. As a child she had thought that she was not lovable enough for her mother. Now, as an adult, she had a better understanding of her mother's part in the distance that existed between them. This understanding may not have led to a more emotionally intimate relationship with her mother in the present, but it did enable her to become aware of how it was affecting her relationship with her daughter. Often a parent's insights into connections between her own childhood and her current relationships with her children will give her the ability to dramatically change her current patterns. Awareness often breaks the connections and provides the parent with a new openness and acceptance of both her child and herself. New relationship possibilities often then emerge.

Jen was assisted in achieving a deeper awareness of her relationship with her daughter because Matt communicated with her with acceptance, curiosity, and empathy rather than with analysis and advice. This enabled Jen to reflect with acceptance, curiosity, and empathy for herself. This gave her the felt sense of safety necessary to reflect in a deeper and more comprehensive manner.

CHAPTER FIVE

Establish PACE

For every child—and every parent too, hopefully—home is where you can relax and feel safe, laugh and cry, hope and dream, and prepare yourself with a mixture of excitement and fear for the adventures and challenges that beckon. Your home is your secure base. When the world has become too stressful or too stimulating, or when you have just been away too long, your home finds its way into your mind and body and back you come to repair, rejuvenate, and recharge. You return home if you are able, and if you cannot return home, thinking about it comforts you. Your home is your safe haven. When home is working at its best, being a secure base and safe haven equally well, it most likely is characterized by qualities of PACE (playfulness, acceptance, curiosity, empathy).

PACE encapsulates an attitude, an interpersonal stance toward one another that cherishes and invites the development of one person without hurting the development of the other. PACE conveys the awareness that there is something special for each of us, for all of us to be here together, creating a sanctuary, that none of us could experience alone. In such a home, the individual is not sacrificed for the family, and the family is not sacrificed for the individual. The rights of all—parents and children—are valued and respected. Parental authority does not imply that the inner life of the parent is valued more than the inner life of the child. The thoughts and feelings, hopes and dreams, memories and intentions, values and beliefs of all are welcomed into the family dialogue, into the family's development. The parents protect and meet the needs of their children. Parents are responsible for ensuring the safety of their children. Parents who are best at this tend to be best at ensuring that their children will feel safe with them. When children feel safe, they are much more likely to accept and be influenced by parental guidance and rules, values and judgments, experiences and intentions. When a child fears that his parent will criticize a certain aspect of himself, he is likely to hide that part of himself and diminish his parent's influence over that part. Fear may increase compliance in the short term, at the cost of decreasing genuine influence in the long term. PACE enhances a child's sense of safety with his parents. At the same time, it helps him to be ready and able to be guided by his parents while still fully developing his own self-reliance abilities.

PACE is based on the attitude, and the inner life, of the parent that appears when she is engaged with her infant in reciprocal play and dialogue. This attitude conveys an open, warm, and inviting stance of unconditional love and joy. With such an attitude, infants develop without effort. Such an attitude is crucial in facilitating attachment security, the parent-child relationship, the rich and comprehensive intersubjective experiences that are beneficial to each, and also to the child's overall development. For many practical, psychological, and cultural reasons, that attitude tends to decrease as the child matures. PACE seems to decrease as parents begin to socialize their toddlers. During socialization, parents tend to think that they need to adopt a more serious and stern tone of voice that involves more than simply getting their child's attention. The voice tone tends to convey the belief that the child's behavior is wrong. The intent seems to be to motivate him to develop more socially appropriate behaviors. This stern tone also frequently implies that the parents are evaluating and correcting their child's thoughts, feelings, and intentions associated with the behaviors.

It is possible that habitually adopting a stern voice does not benefit socialization, but may actually be detrimental to it. Such a voice tone does not encourage reciprocity and thus does not facilitate intersubjectivity, which may be the most effective form of socialization that human beings possess. However, reducing this serious, annoyed, nonverbal tone during discipline is not as easy to do as you might think. Parents have socialized their children that way for generations and any significant change toward a more open and reciprocal stance is likely to require substantial reflection and practice.

The parental attitude of PACE communicates to the child a core affective tone that the parent is experiencing toward him. This enables the child to respond to the parent from a place of safety and openness, accepting the intersubjective experience that is unfolding. When a child is very receptive to his parent's experience, he is much more receptive to her acts of discipline. When a parent is very receptive to her child's experience, the child will be very receptive to hers. With greater emphasis on PACE there is less need for problem solving, rules and consequences, and forced compliance. Discipline flows naturally from the parent-child relationship and may actually enhance it, rather than being a threat to it. I will now present each of the four components of PACE in some detail.

Playfulness

It is frequently hard to be engaged with an infant without being playful. When an infant is in the quiet and alert state of consciousness, he wants to be interacting with his parent. However, he does not seek lectures; he wants to play. He wants the interactions to be characterized by rhythms, movements, and laughter, with exaggerated facial expressions and variations in voice inflections and tones that we call a singsong voice. He wants the soothing and ongoing presence that comes from repetition, and he also wants periodic surprises in the parent's expressions. Most parents know how to maintain their infant's attention. They intuitively engage with him in the way that he wants—playfully.

There is energy in this engagement between parent and infant that truly seems to bring the infant to life, and his parent along with him.

A well-known infant researcher, Daniel Stern, calls this vitality affect, which characterizes the background affective tone that is so evident in these interactions. He measured this affect by its intensity and rhythm. As he studied these moving and continuous affective states, he discovered that most parents intuitively matched the infant's state with a synchronized affective state of their own. Both parent and child were in the same rhythm, and the intensity of their expressions was quite similar. He noted that the infant preferred this matched state over states that were out of sync. The parents in the study did as well. This matched affective state between parent and infant became known as attunement and it came to be considered fundamental to the developing relationship and to the development of the infant. The most frequent state of attunement between parent and infant involves playfulness.

Much of the communication between a parent and a young child is centered on playfulness. Nursery rhymes, peekaboo, hide-and-seek, and the game of "I'm-gonna-get-you" cause excitement and laughter, during which the infant and parent are communicating their wishes, feelings, and intentions. Words gradually emerge in the context of smiling and experiencing joy and mutual interest. Much of this occurs prior to the onset of discipline or when playfulness is the primary interaction and discipline is still secondary.

These early months and years of joint playfulness have many benefits:

1. The primary shared emotions are joy and interest, excitement and happiness.
2. In those moments, the relationship is characterized by acceptance and openness to each other.
3. The infant learns to regulate positive emotions by being matched with the parent in the underlying vitality affect.
4. The infant is developing shared interests and a joint history with the parent.
5. The infant is expanding his attention and concentration by being kept in the activity through the attention and concentration of the parent.
6. The infant is discovering very positive traits about self and parent through these moments of fun and laughter.

7. The infant and parent are discovering a depth of unconditional love and safety that will be very helpful during the stressful acts of discipline that lie ahead.

8. The infant is discovering the value and enjoyment of experiencing this reciprocal, cooperative stance.

Playfulness between parent and child continues to serve these valuable relationship and developmental goals throughout childhood when the parent recognizes its value and incorporates it into the daily routines of life.

Developing Playfulness

Frequent reciprocal laughter is often one sign of a playful attitude. Laughter is a great antidote to shame and fear, and when they are laughing, both parent and child tend to feel safe and accepted. Laughter builds memories of unconditional acceptance of each other, an acceptance that underlies any differences or problems. When laughing, parent and child tend to experience each other and the relationship itself as being special, as more than good enough. These experiences build a safety net that enables both parent and child to better manage future conflicts and separations. Often playfulness and gentle teasing become an important means whereby parent and child are able to accept and gently address traits of each other that tend to cause conflicts. Say a Dad obsesses about checking everything twice before the family gets in the car and as a result becomes a bit irritable. If he is able to laugh at himself and accept some gentle teasing about this trait, his family will be more able to accept his quirk and manage the added demand without becoming seriously upset. The trip then gets off to a much better start. The joint playful tone communicates that the relationship is bigger than any small, irritating traits of any family member. This acceptance, in turn, tends to reduce such traits.

Humor assists children in developing another perspective on events. Humor enables a person to see an event from another position and to hesitate—and be open to the other's experience—before concluding that he knows the meaning of an event. Humor enables a child to see that an event may not be all bad and to be aware of positive features of situations that otherwise might be overlooked.

While laughing, gentle teasing, and telling funny stories certainly qualify as playfulness, they are not necessary for the parent and child to be engaged playfully. Playfulness, as the child grows older and the relationship becomes more familiar, often has a quality of lightness and openness to what is happening and what might happen next. There is no agenda. The parent and child are together, maybe playing a game, maybe going for a walk. There is a meandering quality to their activities. Each is welcoming the other into his or her presence, sharing personal experience and being open to the experience of the other. The intent in the activity is simply to provide a temporary space and time for their interactions together. Their primary intent is simply to be together, to enjoy each other's company. During those moments together, nothing else matters. Any conflicts, responsibilities, and frustrations are set aside. These playful times are truly moments of deepening, broadening, and healing for the ongoing relationship. They are moments when each becomes absorbed by the other. When such moments occur, they are not likely to be forgotten, and whatever conflicts occur in the future are experienced within a context that holds onto the relationship that exists under the conflict.

The lightness and openness of playfulness are important qualities to try to maintain when engaged in routine day-to-day activities. These qualities bring both parent and child into the present more fully while at the same time grounding them in the unconditional quality of their relationship. This playful quality helps to keep things within the perspective of the important things in their relationships, their larger goals, and their lives stretching into the future. This quality enables parent and child not to take things too seriously. When the child makes a mistake, the parent is also able to experience his successes. When the child has a problem, it is seen in the context of his strengths. When parents impose "unfair" discipline, this is often seen as unnecessary but well intentioned. The joy and happiness from being parent and child, from being together is always in the background, making any problem so much more easily faced and resolved. One father told me about a conflict with his 7-year-old son, who called him a "mean old man." Later that day, the boy told his father that he loved him. The father reminded him about what he had said earlier and asked if he had changed his mind. The boy replied, "Oh no, Dad, you are a mean old man. But I love you anyway."

One mom had an 8-year-old boy, Sam, who was untidy, as many 8-year-olds are. While passing through the dining room, she saw his jacket half on the chair, so she hollered to him in the family room to come out and hang it up. She heard him moan something about a TV show, so she smiled and took the coat herself. Half an hour later she called her son and husband for dinner. As they entered the kitchen, they noticed Sam's jacket hanging from a hook above the window where plants usually hung.

Sam: Mom!
Mom: What? [totally innocent]
Sam: Why did you do that?
Mom: What?
Sam: Put my coat up there.
Mom: I thought I'd help you out, and I was on my way to the kitchen, so there it ended up.
Dad: You are some help.
Mom: Hey, I didn't see you helping Sam out when he had trouble getting his jacket put away.
Dad: Hey, I hung up my coat.
Mom: Good thing too. I have a special spot ready for it if you don't.
Dad: And where would that be?
Mom: Might be in the garage . . . might be next door at George's house.
Dad: You wouldn't dare.
Sam: Mom is crazy, Dad. You better not say that.
Mom: You tell him, son. He better not. Hey, what's this about me being crazy?
Sam: You are! No other mom would hang up her kid's jacket above the kitchen window.
Mom: Do you mean other kid's moms don't help them the way I help you?

Sam: Some help!

Mom: You'll appreciate it someday.

Playfulness and Repair

The following suggestions involve playfulness in improving the quality of the attachment.

Admit Mistakes

Parents who can admit mistakes are likely to be able to not take themselves or their mistakes too seriously and to be able to laugh about them. This models for the child how to respond to a mistake and also encourages the parents to have the same attitude toward their child's mistakes that they have toward their own mistakes.

For example, a father had stepped away from the table for a moment and when he came back he saw that his son was eating dessert.

Dad: I told you to finish your meal before getting your pie! [Silence follows. The boy looks at his empty plate on the counter, and then at his father, and his father sees it too.]

Dad: Oops! [Taking his own plate and putting it in front of his son.] I meant to say that you had to eat what was left on my plate before getting your pie!

Boy: [after staring at his father's plate for a moment] Does that mean that you cannot have your pie until your plate is clean?

Dad: I guess so.

Boy: Well, I only have room for my pie, Dad! Sorry, I can't help.

Dad: [laughs] Okay, you win! I should have looked at your plate before saying anything about your eating your pie. You caught me. Sorry!

Boy: That's okay, Dad, but you still can't have your pie until you finish your meal.

Keep an Open Mind

It is helpful to have the ability to see humor in situations that on the surface may be upsetting. When a parent is able to suspend judgment about a child's motives for his behavior, the parent is more likely to be able to see incongruities between a child's intentions and the behavioral results and then to be less distressed about the behavior. This will leave room for seeing the situation with some humor.

A man came home to find that his lawn had not been mowed, though he had told his son that it needed to be done before dinner. Rather than assuming that his son had forgotten his responsibility and then scolding him, the dad realized that he first needed to understand his son's reason for not mowing the lawn.

> *Dad*: I notice that the grass isn't cut. What's up?
> *Son*: There wasn't any gas in the can!
> *Dad*: Didn't I tell you that if you ran out of gas, I wanted you to use the scissors?

If Dad has assumed that his son was being defiant and then scolded him, a strain on the relationship would have developed that would preclude humor and closeness. Refusing to judge a child's motives based on our own assumptions, but rather asking the child about them often reduces conflict and increases successful communication.

Keep It Light When Possible

Parents who can maintain a playful attitude will quickly discover that when they address misbehavior, their child is likely to be less defensive and more willing to accept responsibility for it. Humor suggests that it is "only behavior," which can be successfully addressed.

For example, Dad comes into the living room to see the TV on, but the schoolbooks untouched.

> *Dad*: I am always amazed when I see that in our house the TV can turn itself on and schoolbooks have pages that stick together and don't open.
> *Daughter*: Yeah, Dad, I've turned the TV off 20 times but it just keeps turning on all by itself!
> *Dad*: And the schoolbook?

Daughter: I tried to open the pages but I was afraid that I
would rip them, so I didn't pull too hard.

Dad: Thanks.

Daughter: No problem, Dad.

Dad: And it's no problem for me too. Come here and I'll see if
I can open your schoolbook for you.

Daughter: That's great, Dad! [Moves from the couch to the
table where his books are.]

Acceptance

It is so easy to accept a newborn. Everything about the baby seems so
precious, so right, that there seems to be no need to evaluate or
change him. His behaviors are easy to accept even when they cause
some difficulties for his parent. The parent knows that he did not in-
tentionally wet his diaper just after it was changed. It is easy not to
evaluate the thoughts, feelings, or motives that underlie his behaviors
since his inner life is barely formed yet. A baby tends to be adorable
just as he is. For the great majority of parents, accepting a baby is just
as easy as loving him, just as natural as breathing.

The infant and older child's safety is enhanced when his inner self
is never at risk for rejection, ridicule, or disappointment, when his
parents relate to him. He is certain that he is accepted completely for
who he is and he always will be, regardless of what the future brings.
This is not to say that his parents will never be angry or disappointed
with his behavior. They will be—many times. Rather, only his behavior is subject to their evaluations and guidance, judgments and criticisms. Who he is never is.

Young children are quick to demonstrate a full range of emotional
expressions in response to various situations. These can range from
excitement and joy to anger, fear, and sadness. Expressions of anger
tend to be the hardest for parents to accept. In one study, parents
who were autonomously (i.e., securely) attached, rather than preoccupied (i.e., ambivalent) or dismissive (i.e., avoidant) attached, were
able to accept their child's anger, whereas those parents in the other
two classifications were not. Securely attached parents were not

threatened by their child's anger. It was not evaluated as being wrong or bad; rather, it was simply one aspect of his person. However, certain angry behaviors would not be accepted, though the anger underlying the behavior would be.

Acceptance, when felt completely and taken for granted, becomes a secure base upon which a child is much more likely to learn from his mistakes and to accept his parents' decisions regarding his behavior. Since his behavior has not undermined his self-worth nor threatened the relationship, he has the freedom to explore his mistake and remain open to why his parents decided that the behavior needed to be changed. With acceptance, he is able to experience his parents' perspective on the behavior and actually be receptive to their guidance—though in the short term he might be frustrated and annoyed.

Acceptance is unconditional. He or she is their child, and there is nothing that he or she could do that would make them wish that it were different. In many homes, parents do not find it difficult to experience such complete acceptance of their infant. Rather they feel thrilled, overjoyed, blessed, and fortunate to have this gift. They spend moments, hours, days, and months actively discovering qualities in their child—qualities that they invariably fall in love with and fully accept.

Acceptance has nothing to do with permissiveness. Behaviors remain to be evaluated and guided. Since a child has much to learn regarding behavior, parents have much that they need to teach him. While limiting or directing his behavior, they nevertheless are continuously demonstrating their acceptance. They do this by focusing their teaching and evaluations on the behavior itself and never upon the child. They do this by not using relationship withdrawal as a means of discipline. There may be consequences for behaviors thought to be poor choices, but these consequences never involve a threat to the relationship or an assessment that there are deficiencies in the self of their child.

Developing Acceptance

At the core of developing and maintaining acceptance of a child is the habit of perceiving the individual child beyond the behaviors.

Separating the child from his behaviors enables a parent to address the behavior while communicating acceptance of the person who engaged in the behavior. In that way, the child himself is always unconditionally accepted, whereas his behavior may or may not be. The assumption is that the behavior represents the child's best effort at the time to respond in the best manner to a situation, balancing various interests, desires, and perceived needs. The parent may disagree with the choice while at the same time accepting the intention behind the choice.

Over the years in my work with families, I have found that I have been most effective when I communicated my confidence that both parents and child were doing the best they could to manage a situation and correct a family problem. Knowing that I knew that they were doing the best they could, both parents and child were more likely to trust that I was not searching for someone to blame. I knew that they were not selfish, mean, or lazy. Their goals were reasonable, though their efforts to attain them might be in error. Interwoven within their goals were their strengths and vulnerabilities. As these emerged, more successful behaviors tended to follow. Without my first communicating acceptance of all present, some would not feel safe. In such a setting, any problem-solving interventions would meet with resistance and eventual noncompliance.

Having confidence in the child's inner life and in the relationship itself makes it easier to maintain acceptance. When certain behaviors undermine this confidence, it is much harder to continue to communicate acceptance of the child. At times this lack of confidence has to do with the parent's doubts about her parenting abilities. If she can address these doubts without shame, she will be in a better position to address the behavior while accepting the child. At other times, the lack of confidence relates more to the apparently severe problems associated with the child's behaviors. In such situations, it is wise to understand the meaning of the behavior first without reacting to it. The child will be much more likely to be engaged with his parent in the process of making sense of his behavior when he feels accepted for who he is. Solutions for the behavioral problems will then be much easier to see.

Obstacles to Acceptance

The following suggestions are intended to increase a parent's acceptance of her child by imaging specific obstacles to acceptance.

Reduce Your Anger

Acceptance is undermined when the parent's anger over the behavior
of the child is intense and lasting. Parents often believe that by showing clear and strong anger at their child, their discipline will be
more effective. In the short term, positive results may seem evident.
In the long term, these results tend to evaporate and the behavior is
more likely to become more entrenched. The parents' response has
brought the behavior into the sphere of the self, and the child is likely
to test that connection. He needs to know, while he fears the answer:
"Does my parent accept me and love me as I am?" "Is she proud of
me, or disappointed that I am her child?" This doubt, and the resulting test, is at the center of repetitive misbehaviors much more than
we think.

The most effective discipline in the long term enables the child to
remain safe in the relationship. Intense anger places this felt sense of
safety at risk. Safety will increase his readiness to learn from the act
of discipline. If discipline is only about his behavior, he is likely to be
quite willing to learn about that. If it is about the inner self, however,
he is likely to become quite oppositional and not very receptive. If
discipline seems directed toward the self, it elicits shame. When it
seems directed toward behavior, it elicits guilt if indicated.

Discipline that includes a brief expression of anger tends to be
much more effective. Such anger is expressed with words that focus
on the behavior, not on the thoughts, emotions, or intentions that
might relate to the behavior. It is restricted to infrequent, serious misbehaviors rather than minor behaviors. Discipline that involves a natural environmental consequence or even no specific consequence at
all tends to be much more effective, as are follow-up comfort, support, and relationship repair. Acts of discipline are best when they do
not threaten the relationship nor the child's sense of self-worth. In
fact, discipline might be a means of confirming the unconditional

strength of the relationship. No matter what the child does, the relationship is intact; the child is still unconditionally accepted. Under those conditions, a child is much more likely to learn from acts of discipline. He remains safe, and he trusts that his parents' motives for placing limits on his behavior are truly in his best interests.

Avoid Negative Judgments

Acceptance is threatened when the parent makes negative judgments about the child's thoughts, emotions, and intentions that led to the behaviors.

Often, when angry about a child's behavior, a parent expresses her anger in a manner that includes assumptions about the child's inner life that led to the behavior. When a parent says, "You just took that money because you always want your way!" her anger and judgment go beyond the child's behavior of taking money and reflect her assumption about his motives for taking it. As soon as her anger is directed at his inner life, he experiences her as not accepting who he is. If she had limited her anger toward his behavior, saying, for example, "I am angry that you took that money," his basic sense of self and their relationship would have remained separate from her anger.

Safeguard the Relationship

The use of relationship withdrawal when a child has done something wrong is an obstacle to communicating acceptance. Parents sometimes combine anger, negative assumptions, and relationship withdrawal as a method of discipline. The relationship withdrawal is seen as a necessary, final component of the discipline to ensure that the child knows that his misbehavior is serious and that the parent is equally serious in ensuring that the behavior does not reoccur. Relationship withdrawal, however, often creates some doubt within the child as to whether or not his parent likes him. The child might even wonder whether the parent is happy that he is her child. The relationship itself becomes less safe. When relationship withdrawal is routinely employed as a discipline technique, attachment security may be compromised, which could then activate further behavioral problems. Even if such problems are not created, routine withdrawal is likely to create a distance in the relationship that will undermine its strength and influence on the child's life in the years ahead.

Accept the Child's Inner Life

A parent may have difficulty accepting her child when he says that he does not like her. Accepting a child's inner life, including a thought or feeling of dislike toward them, is a very challenging situation for most parents. The parent is likely to feel that the child is unfair, selfish, or mean. However, his dislike is not a behavioral event; it is an experience. An experience is not right or wrong, bad or good, fair or unfair; it simply is. If the parent accepts his experience as it is, he is more likely to express it appropriately and not in inappropriate actions. By accepting it, the parent is more likely to be able to be curious about its roots, what else is associated with it, and her child's attitude toward it. For instance, does he wish he did not dislike his mother or is he glad that he does?

Acceptance is directed toward the person's inner life, involving his thoughts, emotions, attitudes, wishes, perceptions, memories, intentions, values, and beliefs. A parent may have different qualities in her own inner life, but she accepts that his are what they are and they are part of who he is, at least in the present. If he says he does not like her, she may certainly place limits and not accept behaviors that reflect his dislike. Knowing that he dislikes her may itself be experienced by her as being painful and unfair. However, by accepting what he says about his feelings, she has an opening toward understanding the factors that are creating his dislike, which may lead to the opportunity to repair the relationship. If she rejects his inner attitude and he has to conceal it, it will be much less likely to be addressed and understood. It will then be more likely to manifest in unacceptable behaviors. Concealing his inner life will make relationship repair much more difficult.

A parent needs considerable psychological strength to accept her child's dislike for her. However, when the parent is able to accept whatever she discovers within his inner life, she can begin to resolve whatever factors led to its development.

For example, John, age 10, was upset because his mother told him that his younger brother could play with the dog outside. He would have to wait until later in the day.

John: But I want to play with him now!

Mom: It's your brother's turn now. Spotty gets too excited if you both play with him.

John: That's not fair! You always let Teddy play with him.

Mom: I said no, John. You can't always have things your way.

John: You're so mean to me! You hate me!

Mom: Wow! Where did that come from?

John: But it's true!

Mom: John . . . wait a second. What did I just say?

John: You said that I always want things my way!

Mom: Oh my! I did, didn't I? That wasn't fair to you, John. I'm sorry.

John: You just don't like me, do you?

Mom: Oh, John, I'm so sorry if I made you think that. And I can see where you might. You're upset because you really want to play with Spotty now and I said no. And you're upset. That's all. Everyone gets upset sometimes when they can't do what they want to do. It doesn't mean that you're selfish, or just think of yourself all the time, or that there is anything wrong with you. I can see where you thought that I think there is something wrong with you for getting upset with me. I am truly sorry, John, and will be more careful what I say to you.

John: I don't think that it always has to be my way.

Mom: I know, John. I made a mistake and should not have said that.

John: Why did you?

Mom: Sometimes I make mistakes. You get annoyed and I don't want to admit sometimes that your annoyance with what I do is okay. Sometimes I think that you shouldn't get annoyed with me and then I guess I find a reason to explain it. And the reason says that there is something wrong with you—and your getting annoyed with me—and there really isn't.

John: So it's okay to be annoyed with you.

Mom: It certainly is, John. I often got annoyed with my mom and dad when they said no about things.

John: And did your mom get upset with you for being annoyed?

Mom: [smiles] I guess she did, a lot. Maybe that's why I do with you too sometimes. I didn't like it when my mother said things like that to me, and now I do the same thing to you! I have to work at this more.

John: I agree.

Mom: So if you want to get annoyed at not being able to play with Spotty now—feel free to do so.

John: No, that's okay. I don't want to play with him now.

Curiosity

There are magic moments when parents discover their infant, and—as I recently learned—when grandparents discover their grandchild. Every movement, facial expression, vocal utterance, and glance—each one unique—is appreciated for the remarkable meaning that it conveys. Each physical characteristic is experienced, again as a unique feature of "my baby," and noted as lovely. Each parent is frequently delighted over who their baby is and is likely to become. Each parent wants to tell the world—since it is difficult to believe that the world would not be equally enthralled—about who they are discovering their baby to be.

Parents, from the moment that they are aware of their infant-still-in-the-womb, find themselves very curious about who their infant is. From birth on, they continuously observe whatever features are evident, including the baby's appearance, movements, physiological rhythms, and where he focuses his eye gaze. They are aware of subtle changes in his activities from day to day, noticing quickly something new and then trying to make sense of it. Often what is new is a sign to the parents of their infant's special qualities and abilities. In essence, parents are continuously involved in acts of discovery of their child, and when they discover something, they allow it to have an impact on them. Their infant, seeing the impact of his actions and expressions on his parents, becomes more aware of these actions and more likely to engage in actions that have a positive impact on his parents. His parents' continuing curiosity about him leads them to make guesses about his inner life that are rooted in his nonverbal expressions. They interact with him in ways congruent with their guesses. Patterns of expressions, guesses, and responses develop that, in essence, go a long way in organizing the inner life of the infant. When the parents perceive their child as having an enthusiastic response to the cat, and they show matching enthusiasm to his interest in the cat, his interest is likely to develop further as he becomes absorbed in the cat. If the parents do not respond to his interest in the cat, it is likely to occur less frequently and to be less recognized and focused on by the infant.

Because of the nature of intersubjective experience, the parents' discovery of the meaning of their infant's features and expressions greatly affects his experience of himself. When parents discover their infant to be delightful, lovable, and interesting, their infant discovers himself to possess those features. However, if a parent finds her infant lazy, mean, or selfish, he will think he has those features. Thankfully, such parental discoveries tend to be much less common, with the exception being parents who were themselves thought to have those features as infants. Most parents, the great majority of the time, discover their infants to be marvelous living beings whom they are desperate to get to know better and better each day.

Developing Curiosity

Difficulties relating to curiosity are more likely to occur as the child becomes older and acts of discipline become a necessary part of day-to-day parent-child interactions. Discipline refers to the necessity of teaching children about behaviors and events that we consider to be safe or not safe, age appropriate or inappropriate, and right or wrong. During acts of discipline, parents often begin to assume that they know the reasons for the child's behaviors. Since the child is doing what the parent does not want the child to do, and since the parent has told the child what is right or wrong a number of times before, the parent often begins to assume that the child's motives for misbehavior were themselves wrong. Parents begin to assume that their child acted in that manner because "he just wanted to get away with it" or "she just was being lazy" or "he's just not trying hard enough."

Acts of discipline begin to replace acts of discovery. Assumptions of negative motives replace assumptions of positive motives. These assumptions replace curiosity about motives. When this occurs—due to the nature of intersubjectivity—children begin to assume that they do have negative motives, thoughts, or feelings. They begin to assume that there is something wrong with who they are. A child begins to sacrifice his view of himself to try to maintain safety in his attachment with his parents. Or he begins to resist his parents' assumptions about his inner life. He begins to oppose their views about him and even threatens the safety of his attachment with them to try to preserve his sense of himself. He tries to convince them that he is not the bad boy that he believes they think he is. Rather than being raised with the confidence that he can be close to his parents and also an independent person himself, he is beginning to believe that he has to choose between self and relationship.

The Nonjudgmental "Why"

Many of these problems may be avoided when parents maintain a strong sense of curiosity about their child's behavior. If they maintain an open, nonjudgmental stance toward their child's inner life, they are likely to provide discipline without the degree of conflict and relationship stress that often occurs. Discipline needs to be directed at behavior, not assumptions about the child's motives. A child can often accept the authority of his parents when it relates to his behavior as long as the authority does not try to change his inner life.

An attitude of curiosity is a "not-knowing" stance that requires that the parent inquire about the child's inner life that led to the behaviors under concern. Such inquiries are much more likely to be successful with an attitude of acceptance of whatever qualities emerge. The child needs to feel safe that his inner life will not be criticized if he is to openly explore it with his parent. When that is the case, and the child's behavior creates distress either for the child or another person, the child is more likely to acknowledge his mistake and modify his behavior. If his inner life is judged, he is more likely to feel shame and attempt to hide from and deny the behavior.

With a not-knowing attitude, a focus on responding appropriately to the behavior itself, the parent is then in an excellent position to accept the situation and manage the behavior. Then the child will be more willing to explore possible factors that led to the behavior, which include the following possibilities:

- Belief that he has to meet his own needs and not rely on others
- Not feeling safe
- Feeling alone
- A sense of shame
- A belief that a situation is hopeless
- Fear of being vulnerable or dependent
- Fear of rejection
- Difficulty self-regulating intense affect—positive or negative
- Difficulty relying on parent to coregulate affect—positive or negative
- Felt sense that his life is too hard
- Feeling that his parents truly do not see and understand him
- Assumptions that parents' motives and intentions are negative
- Lack of confidence in own abilities
- Lack of confidence that parent will comfort or assist during hard times
- Unwillingness to allow himself to seek or receive comfort
- Inability to understand why the parent does things
- Need to deny inner life because of frightening affect that exists there
- Inability to express inner life even if he wanted to
- Fear of failure
- Fear of trusting happiness or success

When parents accept their child, these aspects of his experience are much more likely to emerge within the intersubjective experience. Parents are then able to join their child in the experience and as it dissipates and becomes integrated into a more coherent sense of self, the behavioral problems are likely to become less or to cease entirely.

Discovering the "Why"

A nonjudgmental, open curiosity about a child's thoughts, feelings, and intentions is likely to facilitate the child's interest in his own inner life, develop his skills in identifying his thoughts, feelings, and intentions, and encourage honest expression of his inner life. This in turn will enable his parents to understand him better and help him feel understood and accepted even when his parents need to limit his behavior.

To communicate such curiosity, the parent might try questions and comments such as the following:

- How does that seem to you?
- Tell me about that.
- What does that mean to you?
- What do you want to happen?
- What do you think about that?
- What kind of feelings do you have now?
- What do you think makes that important to you?
- If you do that, what do you expect to happen next?
- I think I understand why you want to do that—any reason for not doing it?
- How do you think it will be for you if it doesn't work out the way you want?
- Will it be hard for you if I don't let you do that?
- You really seem to be looking forward to that!
- How long have you been planning that?
- Wonder how it will be if you are not able to do that?
- I think I understand what this means to you. Am I missing anything?

It is important that such comments and questions be expressed with a nonverbal stance of acceptance and openness. It is equally important that the parent truly listen to her child's response. Her intention is to understand, not to find an opening to change her child's mind and justify a decision that she has already made. Children are quite sensitive to their parents' intentions and will know quickly if the parents are truly curious or are simply "reasoning" with them so that their own thoughts and intentions can dominate. Curiosity requires that a parent is truly open to being influenced by the inner life of her child who she is trying to understand.

Curiosity is equally important when directed toward positive experiences and behaviors that the child is demonstrating. The parent is conveying that she is not interested only in problems and vulnerabilities; she is also interested in his interests and strengths. She is interested in all of her child. She does not take his strengths for granted. She does not overlook him when he is doing well. She is constantly finding reasons for delighting in him, enjoying him, being amazed at who he is and who he is becoming. By her perception of—and response to—these qualities of his inner life, he will be more aware of them himself. He is likely to take greater pride in those features of himself and develop them further.

These acts of discovery need to be fluid and continuously open. If they are rigid, the child may experience an obligation or pressure to meet his parent's expectation that he think or feel a certain way or be interested in certain things or activities. Then he would believe that he has no room to develop and change or his parents might be annoyed, frustrated, or more distant from him. For example, they may discover that he loves playing basketball and is quite good at it. They expect him to play on the school team and when he decides to draw and paint in his free time, they are confused and disappointed. They had already created a vision of their son being a popular school athlete and he is turning his back on their vision. What originally was delight in his pleasure in playing basketball now has become a disappointment in his pleasure in artwork. In such circumstances the child is not likely to feel supported and understood and is more likely to begin to hide his hopes and dreams.

For example, Chris, age 9, had lost interest in riding his bike after school. His mother was puzzled by this since he really had seemed to enjoy riding his bike, and because he did not seem to be replacing it with anything else. He just sat and moped after school.

Mom: Hey, Chris, what's up?
Chris: Nothing much.

Mom: Yeah, I noticed that lately. Seems like you don't feel like doing much of anything. Not even riding your bike.

Chris: I guess.

Mom: How come?

Chris: I don't know.

Mom: I noticed that you seem a little sad lately . . . a little down.

Chris: I'm okay.

Mom: The way you said, "I'm okay" makes me think that you are not as okay as you usually are.

Chris: I guess not.

Mom: Any ideas?

Chris: I don't know.

Mom: What's that like—not knowing?

Chris: What do you mean?

Mom: Oh, if you're not feeling great and you don't know why—what's it like not knowing why?

Chris: I don't know.

Mom: So you don't know that either. That must be hard. Like your mind is covered in fog and you don't know why. Must get tiring having fog cover your mind like it has been lately. Has the fog been there long?

Chris: I guess.

Mom: That's what I thought. I wonder where it came from.

Chris: I don't know.

Mom: Yeah, when fog gets in my mind I often don't know where it comes from either. I do notice, though, that sometimes it comes to help me not notice something in my mind that I don't want to think about. It's trying to be my friend.

Chris: What do you mean?

Mom: Sometimes I think the fog tries to help me not think about something that is bothering me. Do you think that's what your fog is trying to do?

Chris: I guess . . . but I wasn't trying to get his dumb dog killed! I wasn't! I didn't even want to play with him! [tears in his eyes]

Mom: What happened, Chris?

Chris: I was riding my bike up the road and this guy, Mr. Mason, was playing with his dog outside. And his dog saw me and started to run over to me. And I saw a car coming and I tried to get him to stop . . . but he kept coming . . . and the car almost hit him . . . and Mr. Mason yelled at me. He said that I wanted to get his dog killed! And I didn't! I wasn't trying to get his dog to run after me. I wasn't, Mom! I wasn't!

Mom: Oh, Chris . . . no wonder you've had the fog try to help you! Mr. Mason said that he thought you wanted to hurt his dog! That you were trying to have him get hit by a car! And that was so painful for you. First, it must have been so scary that his dog was almost hit by the car . . . so scary, since I know how much you love animals. Second, that Mr. Mason would think that you would do that on purpose—try to get his dog hurt—how much that must have hurt you that he would think that about you! A wonderful boy who loves dogs! How unfair Mr. Mason was.

Chris: Do you think so, Mom?

Mom: Yes, I think so, Chris. I think that Mr. Mason does not know you the way that I know you. If he did, he would know that you would never do anything that would hurt his dog or any dog. Never!

Chris: I wouldn't, Mom!

Mom: I know that about you, son. I know that more than anything!

Chris: Why would he do that, Mom? Why would he say that about me?

Mom: I don't know, Chris. Maybe he was scared, and when he's scared he might say things without thinking. Maybe he felt that it was his fault that he wasn't keeping his dog closer or didn't have him on a leash. Maybe he was ashamed of what he didn't do to keep his dog safe and he had to find someone else to blame. Maybe that's it.

Chris: That's not fair, Mom.

Mom: No it's not, son. No it's not. Whatever his reason, he was wrong and never should have pretended that he knew that you tried to make his dog run to you so that he would get hurt. He didn't know that because it's just not true!

Chris: It's not, Mom.

Mom: I know that because I know who you are, and you are not a boy who would do something like that!

Chris: I'm not, Mom.

Mom: No, you're not [embracing him]. And do you know what? Maybe you don't need that fog anymore.

Chris: I don't think I do.

Empathy

The affective states of infants are so immediate, so clear, and so contagious. Whether an infant is communicating joy or fear, his parent is likely to immediately feel it with him. She easily shares and expands his positive affects while providing comfort and support for his negative affects. Thus she enables her infant to begin to identify and regulate his various affective states. When the infant's parent is with him in his affect, it is manageable. The infant is also not alone when he experiences his parent's empathy for him. Through the experience of shared affect, the infant is aware that his parent is available, sensitive, and responsive to him.

When communicating empathy to her infant, the parent exaggerates her nonverbal expression of her experience of his affective states. To communicate that she is with him, she uses very clear expressions of her face, rhythms and inflections in her voice, as well as gestures and posture. For example, when her infant looks at her, smiles, and makes vocal sounds, her facial and vocal expression match his while her entire upper body moves in time, with the rhythm and intensity of his voice. The infant experiences her empathy through her nonverbal expressions that are attuned with his expressions.

As the child becomes older, his parent also uses words to communicate empathy, but these words always have a clear nonverbal component that conveys the parent's readiness to join the child in his emotional state. She has the intention of assisting her child to manage the experience, no matter how stressful. Such assistance is given not by fixing a problem or rescuing her child, but rather by simply being present and in the event with him. Her caring and understanding presence enables the child to maintain a more confident stance in the face of the distress. He is not facing it alone.

Through empathy the parent is able to join in her child's experience and share it with him. She has not just become aware of his experiences. She experiences them within herself. Now the child feels "felt" by his parent and is likely to be more comfortable with whatever affective tone and emotion are associated with the event. If the event was stressful for the child, as he communicates with her about it and experiences her affective presence, the stress becomes less. She is holding a part of it. Her affectively regulated presence makes it easier for him to regulate whatever emotion emerges. Getting in sync with her affective tone, he is able to ride on the same rhythm that she is expressing and so manage the distress much more easily.

When a child experiences his parents' empathy for him, he is often able to manage very difficult situations without becoming dysregulated through the experience of intense anger, fear, discouragement, or shame. When parents experience their child's negative emotional states with him, these states get smaller. When parents experience their child's positive emotional states with him, these states get larger.

This empathy must be conveyed clearly with both nonverbal and verbal expressions. Through nonverbal communication, the parent is conveying that she gets it. She has a deep sense of what the child is experiencing and he knows it. She is communicating that she senses his sadness, fear, or anger and she both accepts it and has confidence in his ability to manage it. If he cannot manage it, she will assist him. Her empathy helps him to feel safe enough to make sense of the event. He is able to reflect on the event more fully and discover both its meaning and his possible responses to it.

The parent is not rescuing him from the event or solving his problem for him. She is conveying that she is with him and that he is capable of managing the situation, even though it is hard. Her confidence in him becomes his confidence in himself. Her empathy for him enables him to have empathy for himself regarding a difficult ordeal. He is likely to be more able to accept himself and the situation and face it with much less frustration, fewer distracting self-critical thoughts, and greater openness to discovering flexible responses that best meet the needs of the situation.

Developing Empathy

Empathy is a natural response to being with another person. Our brains are wired to experience empathy for others. If we have experienced empathy from our attachment figures, it is easy to access empathy for those who see us as attachment figures. We easily have empathy for our children when our parents also showed empathy for us. When we fail to experience empathy for our child, it is often because we are distracted by other things on our minds that we think might be more beneficial to the child, including problem solving, teaching, correcting, fixing, or rescuing. If we can delay those responses, see them as having little or no value at that time, then the way is cleared to allow empathy to emerge. Then being aware of it and allowing it to express itself is often all it takes to be with our child empathically.

It is important that the parent be comfortable with the emotions that the child is experiencing. As the parent facilitates her own emotional development, she is also increasing her readiness to experience empathy for her child when he needs it.

Obstacles to Empathy

Regretfully, too often parents do not have confidence that empathy will be that helpful. Rather, they try to fix the problem, give advice, or eliminate the problem by dealing with it themselves. At times, parents will minimize the problem by giving reasons why the child should really not have to worry about it. Parents may understand the value of empathy but not demonstrate it in their day-to-day life with their child.

Parents may not express empathy because they were not raised with empathy and so do not intuitively know how beneficial the experience can be. It is hard to experience empathy for others if we have not experienced empathy from others in the past.

Parents may trust more in the power of reason in assisting their child, since that may be how they were raised and since that is the guiding principle for many child-rearing manuals. While reason may be helpful, it tends to become effective only after the child first feels understanding, comfort, and acceptance. Empathy facilitates those experiences. Also, in stressing reason, parents often imply that the solution was actually quite easy and the child could have thought of it. Or that now that he knows a method for managing the problem, he certainly should not have the same problem in the future. Then, if he does, he is likely to keep it hidden from his parents, being ashamed that he did not follow their advice.

For example, a 14-year-old girl Beth came home from school quite upset that her teacher chose another girl for the lead in the class play when Beth had wanted the role very much.

Beth: Dad, it's just not fair. I really wanted to have the lead!

Dad: I can tell. You really worked at getting it.

Beth: I did, Dad, I really did! Gail didn't try nearly as hard as I did!

Dad: Seems like that makes it even harder that you didn't get the role.

Beth: Yeah, that's why I don't think it was fair. I was better than her!

Dad: So if you thought that she had tried hard and seemed to be as good as you are, it would be easier to take.

Beth: Yeah, I'd be okay, then. I would be disappointed, but I'd deal with it.

Dad: I see. It's a lot more than not getting the part. It's trying to make sense of why you didn't get it. And not being able to figure it out.

Beth: That's it! I could live with it if I thought it were fair! But it's not! I think that Mrs. Jacobson just likes her more than me.

Dad: Wow! If that's how you make sense of it . . . if it seems that she only got the part because she likes her more than you—if that is how it seems to you, I can really understand how upset you are about this.

Beth: Why would she do that, Dad? Why would she be so unfair?

Dad: If that's the reason that she got the part, that she just liked her more . . . it would make it hard to understand. I don't know, Beth I don't know.

Beth: It can't be anything else!

Dad: So it seems to you that's the only possibility.

Beth: Yeah, I wish I knew for sure why she picked her. Then maybe I could forget it.

Dad: I could see how that would make it easier, especially if her reason made sense to you and seemed fair to you. I can see that.

Beth: It would.

Dad: How will it be for you if you never know what her reasons were?

Beth: I don't know, Dad. I always liked Mrs. Jacobson.

Dad: Ah! Even more complicated . . . more confusing.

Beth: It is, Dad, it really is.

Dad: Beth, you seem to be really struggling with this, trying to make sense of it, while still trying to manage how disappointed you are over not getting the part. You really have a lot that you're dealing with!

Beth: Yeah, it's hard.

Dad: It really is, and you're facing it, struggling with it. You're showing a lot of strength, Beth.

Beth: But it still bothers me, Dad.

Dad: I know. I know.

If Beth's dad had tried to help her solve the problem by following a particular course of action, more than likely Beth would not have continued to talk and would not have felt support from her dad to manage her strong emotions regarding what had happened. Also in this example, there really was never any helpful suggestion to make, no advice to give that would not distract from what Beth was doing to manage the situation. She simply needed to have someone with her, without judgment, solutions, or anger about the situation.

PACE, With Love

Love is thought to be the most fundamental feature of the parent-child relationship. Without love, the underlying intention behind parent-child interactions becomes unclear and the relationship is at risk to be temporary. With love, the most fundamental intention for the interactions is now evident and brings safety to the relationship as well as protection and repair after conflicts and separations. Originally, when I spoke of "the attitude" I used the acronym PLACE, including love with the other four traits. I now see love as the underlying feature of the entire relationship, which should be thought of separately.

For the purpose of this work, love is described simply as comprising commitment and enjoyment. Commitment remains present through better and worse, easy and hard. It conveys confidence and trust that no matter what happens, parents will remained committed to their child. The parents will be available, sensitive, and responsive whenever their child needs them. Parents will repair their relationship with their child whenever it is necessary. While parents may divorce each other and end their marital commitment, their love for their child will never end. In this way their child will come to trust them, feel safe and knowing that they will make decisions based upon his best interests.

If parents routinely use relationship withdrawal as a means of discipline, their child may develop doubts about their commitment to him, thus reducing his attachment security and placing him at some risk for various developmental problems. If their anger seems to be directed at his person—rather than his behavior—the doubts are likely to be stronger. If parents periodically threaten their child with abandonment and rejection, his doubts are likely to be even more extensive and the risk to his development even greater. Any short-term benefit of such responses to misbehavior is likely to be lost over the long term. Any short-term benefit is also likely to have too great a cost to the relationship and to the child's development of a coherent and positive sense of self.

By providing the safety that comes from an unconditional permanent commitment, parents are sparing their child the need to continuously test the relationship by engaging in oppositional behaviors. Such safety does not decrease a child's motivation to be good or do the right thing. Rather, when the relationship is experienced as safe and permanent, children are more likely to openly and consistently imitate their parents' inner lives and behaviors. They more often desire to be like their parents and want to impress their parents with the way they live their lives and make their decisions. Through the safety that comes from commitment, children are more ready to develop the skills necessary to be self-reliant someday. At the same time, the child is not likely to become an angel. Being safe, he knows that his own interests, thoughts, and emotions have value and he is likely to assert his own perspective even when his parent's perspective differs. He knows that while his parent may question or limit his behavior, his perspective is still valued and the relationship is in no danger. With unconditional commitment, mild to moderate differences and conflicts come and go, while severe conflicts that imperil the relationship are much less likely to occur.

Reciprocal enjoyment complements commitment to bring love to life and to make love more deeply meaningful and satisfying. With enjoyment, the child becomes aware that the commitment is not a duty, a parental job or responsibility, but rather reflects the fact that his parents truly like him—like him deeply—and want to do things with him, share and develop experiences with him, and come to know him as their unique child. With enjoyment, the child truly experiences that his parents find him to be delightful, lovable, and unique. The child then is much more able to find positive qualities in himself when his parents enjoy who he is.

With commitment, parents are responsive to their child's needs. With enjoyment, parents initiate things with their child. They want to be with him, in part because they enjoy him. Very quickly this becomes primarily a reciprocal process. As parents enjoy being with the child, their child enjoys being with them. This quality of enjoyment truly helps children experience reciprocity. Reciprocal enjoyment also empowers the child to experience positive qualities in himself. He has the power to elicit these positive responses within his parents. Something about him evokes these parental responses. Without enjoyment, a child is at risk to experience himself as not being special enough to evoke a smile or laugh or a desire to be together from his parents. He enters the room, but his parent's face does not light up and her voice does not come to life. Without enjoyment—experienced routinely enough to make it seem real and predictable—love remains important because of commitment, but it becomes hollow and is no longer transforming.

Clearly, parents do not consistently enjoy their child in the same manner that they consistently are committed to him. Following a series of especially challenging or oppositional behaviors from their child, most parents are likely to not enjoy interacting with him for awhile. At other times, for reasons totally unrelated to the child, parents may not experience enjoyment of their child, nor of anyone or anything else. Parents may become depressed, overwhelmed by responsibilities, or preoccupied by other matters. At those times it is unlikely that reciprocal enjoyment is significantly present. This is not a threat to the relationship when it is a minor feature of the relationship, when the parent is able to provide information about the reasons for lack of enjoyment, and when the child has every reason to be confident that the lack of enjoyment will be short-lived. What the child needs to be aware of at those times is that the parent is committed to having the experience of mutual enjoyment return. The parent is not content—nor resigned—to having the relationship remain distant and be an obligation rather than a source of joy. The parent demonstrates that her child is very important to her and she is committed to making reciprocal enjoyment return as soon as possible.

For example, Sam's dad often played a game of pool with him in the evening after dinner. When Sam asked him to play one evening, he refused.

Sam: Hey, Dad, how about a game of pool?
Dad: Not tonight, Sam.
Sam: Ah, Dad, just one!
Dad: I said no. Maybe tomorrow. [mildly annoyed that his son asked him again]
Sam: [Walks away with clear disappointment.]

Dad: Sam, come here a second. I'm sorry that I snapped at you. It has nothing to do with you. Mr. Johnson gave me some work to do tonight, so I have to focus on that. I'm really annoyed with him, not you. Sorry I took it out on you.

Sam: So you have homework! [laughs]

Dad: You could say that.

Sam: Sorry, Dad, you can't play pool until after you finish your homework. [laughs]

Dad: Just one game? [laughs]

Sam: Nope, not till your homework is done.

In summary, PACE represents the characteristics of a parental attitude that create safety and emotional intimacy, openness and delight within the parent-child relationship. It provides a context in which any conflicts or behavioral problems can find an easier resolution. It provides a balance whereby affective and reflective abilities are primed to respond in enjoyable or stressful situations. Most important, it enables the parent to perceive her child beyond any challenging or worrisome behaviors, and to experience her child's permanent place in her mind and heart. Because of the magic of intersubjectivity, mixed with love, PACE enables the relationship to truly transform both parent and child.

CHAPTER SIX

Communicate

Our ability to communicate with members of our family lies at the core of both our development and our family relationships. A child's ability to communicate with his parents enables him to be safe, to learn, to cooperate, to be understood, and to understand others. It enables him to have an influence on others and be influenced by them. It enables him to become aware of his own inner life, including his thoughts, feelings, wishes, and intentions, as well as the inner lives of others. As all of these skills are developing—which they are doing rapidly during the first months of life—the infant is not able to use words to communicate. But the infant is communicating, and he desperately needs someone to communicate with.

With infants, since we cannot use words, we tend to exaggerate our nonverbal expressions to make our thoughts, feelings, and intentions as clear as possible. There is a very distinctive way in which we talk with infants that is known as infant-directed speech or "motherese." Such communication "is organized in repeated phrases, and tends to create slowly changing, cyclic narratives of emotion" (Aitken & Trevarthen, 2001, p. 8). It is these "narratives of emotion" that are the essence of reciprocal communication with our infant. As we join our infant in these pulsating beats and rhythms of energy, he senses that we understand his experience while at the same time we are cocreating the experience. The experience itself and its meaning would be drastically different if his parents did not participate in it. While these cyclic narratives gradually encompass reflective qualities and memories as the child matures, they still require a core of shared affect if they are to reach deeply into the sense of self that began to emerge and become organized during infancy.

Developing Communication

Conversation patterns between parent and child develop naturally as the child matures. The following suggestions present ways to enhance communication and thus improve the quality of the child's attachment to his parents.

Nonverbal Communication

We place so much emphasis on verbal communication that we overlook the central role of nonverbal communication in our relationships and lives. The nonverbal is so pervasive that we stop seeing it. At times we convince ourselves that our influence with our children needs words, presented as superior knowledge, often in the format of a lecture. We think that we have successfully influenced our children when they reply in words, choosing the words that we want to hear so that we will think that they both understand and agree to follow our advice. We often doubt that such communications are sufficient, but we do not know what to add or what to replace the lectures with in order to have a greater influence on our children. So our lectures continue, each one less effective than the last.

The nonverbal aspects of communication—the manner of eye contact and facial expressions, the voice tones and rhythms, the animated and flowing gestures—convey much more of the overall content of our communication than does the verbal component. They convey more of our core thoughts, feelings, and intentions than do our words. Discrepancies between verbal and nonverbal components are almost always decided in favor of the nonverbal. When our partner raises her voice and says, "I am not angry!" we most certainly will conclude that she is angry but has reasons not to acknowledge it verbally.

The nonverbal aspects of communication convey the nuances of our inner life, the unique qualities of our sadness or confusion or excitement in ways that words so often fail to do. Our nonverbal responses also demonstrate a more accurate understanding of the inner life of the other than words do. Our sense that we understand and are understood by the other is much stronger when we utilize nonverbal expressions of our inner lives.

Words themselves, when written, and especially in e-mail, are often ambiguous and lead to miscommunication. The nonverbal component is crucial if the intent of the communication is to be clear. Consider the meanings implied in the following sentence, depending upon where the vocal emphasis is given:

- "*I* didn't say that you were stupid." (But others did.)
- "I didn't *say* that you were stupid." (But I thought it.)
- "I didn't say that *you* were stupid." (But I said your friend was.)
- "I didn't say that you were *stupid*." (But I said that you were foolish.)

Similarly, a child is likely to react one way when his parent yells in anger, "Why did you do that?" He is likely to react quite differently when the parent says in an open, curious, and nonjudgmental way, "Why did you do that?" The parent's affective state, intentions, and assumptions about the child's motives are communicated in large part by the nonverbal component of her speech. Parents are often encouraged not to use the word *why* when talking with their child. There is nothing inherently wrong with that word. The problem occurs when its nonverbal expression communicates annoyance as well as the parent's expectation and even insistence that the child actually knows why and must tell her.

When there is a singsong quality to our vocal expressions, they tend to maintain our attention and convey a relaxed affective tone. There is also a storytelling component to such expressions that holds the attention, builds the interest, and channels the affect of the listener while conveying the intentions of the speaker and the individuals being discussed. This storytelling tone invites the listener to be actively engaged in the story, and in significant ways to actually cocreate the story. Storytelling has been a central way of teaching the young about the self and the larger culture for centuries. There is a continuous form of expression that joins the parent-infant communication with that of all members of the culture.

As child-rearing has come to emphasize the development of the child's reasoning and problem-solving skills, parents have increasingly sought to influence their children by teaching them such skills. Such teachings have focused on presenting the child with a lecture that conveys what is right or wrong, while expecting the child's understanding and agreement.

A lecture might be a better way of presenting objective realities such as the nature of gravity—though one might easily argue with that idea—but it clearly is inferior to the story when speaking of the subjective realities that comprise our affective and social lives. Focusing on compliance and objective knowledge, we conclude that our child agrees with us when, in fact, our child is often simply either using the quickest means of ending the lecture or is truly complying with our thoughts and intentions at the price of failing to develop his own. With lectures we are actually educating our child to comply with authority rather than to develop his own meaning about an issue or event. The disadvantage of compliance is that it tends not to last, or, if it lasts, it tends to be applied without regard to changing circumstances. It may be given to someone else in authority whose values and goals may not be in the best interest of our child. It is better by far to help our child to become competent in determining the merits of a given person or situation, with our own values and goals having become integrated with—but not identical to—his own.

The storytelling tone also conveys an attitude of acceptance of the listener, rather than evaluation and criticism. Such acceptance encourages a nondefensive response. The implied message is that the listener will not be threatened nor criticized. The speaker is conveying his experience and is interested in understanding the experience of the listener. The listener, in turn, senses the open, nonjudgmental tone and becomes engaged in the communication. It is now a conversation, with both speaker and listener contributing to the dialogue. In storytelling, all of the words may come from the storyteller, but the nonverbal communication is definitely reciprocal, and to that extent the listener has an influence on the development of the story.

Communication with children—in fact most of what is entailed in raising a child with an attachment focus—involves engaging our children in conversations, in telling stories together. These conversations focus on sharing our affective states, our focus of attention on common interests, as well as our wishes and intentions toward each other. These conversations convey the understanding that our relationship is based on reciprocal dialogue, on give-and-take that involves each understanding and having empathy for the other as well as each being understood and experiencing such empathy from the other. Such reciprocity does not weaken parental authority; rather, it enhances it. Children much more fully accept and respect their parents' authority when they have confidence in a relationship that is based upon such mutual understanding and empathy. They realize that their parents' vast experience in the world gives them a more reasoned perspective on what is the best response in a given situation. Within attachment security too, they realize that their parents' motives in providing guidance are based on their commitment to the best interests of the child.

The nonverbal aspects of communication focus on the experience of the behavior or event rather than the simple fact of the behavior or event itself. Nonverbal expressions may communicate our interest in, acceptance of, and empathy for the other's experience of the situation. Nonverbal expressions may also communicate our criticism, negative assumptions, and evaluations about how the other experienced the situation. In the former, the child is able to address the behavior and its consequences without threat to the self. The child can learn from the situation without any threat to the relationship. In the latter, the child is likely to feel an attack against the self and a threat to the relationship. In that context, he is less likely to learn.

Sometimes parents have a stern, critical voice tone when disciplining their children. Such a tone immediately creates a tense and defensive stance in the child. No matter how often the parent says, "I like you. I just don't like what you did!" the child is more likely to respond to the tone than the words. A more relaxed, matter-of-fact tone is likely to enable the child to be confident that the parent's critical judgment only involves his behavior.

Verbal Communication

While stressing the necessary foundation of nonverbal communication, it is important not to forget the verbal component. Words convey meanings that the nonverbal cannot achieve. Words take the parent and child beyond the here and now, to memories, plans for the future, and generalizations about events, beliefs, and values. Words enable both parent and child to clarify their intentions and avoid miscommunications. They are necessary to make clear the reasons for performing an action, for holding a thought, or experiencing an emotion.

As the child matures, he naturally develops a receptive vocabulary that is followed fairly rapidly by a smaller expressive vocabulary. As he becomes proficient with verbal communication, he is certainly more able to express with clarity aspects of his inner life. However, in addition to communicating with his parents, the child begins to talk to himself about his inner life. He can use words to help himself understand vague tendencies, sensory states, affective states, sources of fear, and interests, as well as the specifics of his desires and plans. Without words, he is not able to identify certain qualities and features of his inner life. He is less able to understand himself. He is less aware of what he wants, thinks, and feels. He has less of a sense of empowerment. He is less able to organize and regulate his thoughts, emotions, and intentions.

The incentive to develop verbal communication certainly is the desire to communicate with our parents. The benefits go far beyond such communication. Attachment security facilities both the child's desire to communicate and his success in doing it well. His parents are actively interested in his inner life. Their interest facilitates his interest. Because of their interest and their verbal proficiency, they frequently ascribe meaning to their young child's nonverbal expressions. They also frequently describe verbally what he is doing, what he is looking at, what he seems to intend to do, and what he seems to feel about the immediate situation. By chatting with him about his expressions, they are providing him with the means to chat with himself about what he is doing. These skills will last a lifetime.

Such verbal communications between the parent and young child have at their core a simple desire to share, to enjoy each other, to communicate interest in each other. Their incentive is less frequently a desire to evaluate, control, criticize, or teach. When those elements occur periodically—a definite minority of the time—they have value and the child tends to be fairly receptive to the parent's input. However, if they dominate parent's communication, they tend to reduce the frequency of communication.

Many parents have developed the habit of making very frequent communications about their child's behavior. The fact that the communications are positive—"good boy," "great job," "good sitting," does not diminish their inhibiting influence. With such ongoing evaluations, the child does not feel as safe as when he is communicating with his parents in an accepting, mutually enjoyable manner. He does not have to focus on whether or not he is right or wrong, good or bad. He can relax and enjoy his interactions with his parents. They are good enough as they are and he does not have to focus on them or worry about obtaining approval. None of us are comfortable in relationships where we are continuously being evaluated, even if the great majority of the evaluations are positive. Most of us are much more comfortable when we are simply accepted as we are.

Reciprocal Communication

Too often communication between parent and child is one-sided, with the parent talking and the child listening. In such "conversations" the parents' role is to advise, guide, or correct and the child's role is to listen, understand, and comply. A parent first decides what is best for her child and, without seeking the child's perspective (including thoughts, feelings, and wishes), presents that decision to the child.

Efforts to develop the decision by first understanding and integrating the child's perspective are not in evidence. Efforts to develop a joint decision are also missing.

The most effective communication involves talking with each other. The thoughts, feelings, and wishes of each are presented and understood by the other and each evolves, hopefully toward consensus. Each is having an impact on the inner life of the other. Each one's perspective is crucial in determining what is in the best interest of both. When no agreement is reached and the parent must decide, the child is much more likely to accept it when his perspective has been seriously considered. When he is certain that his parent understands and accepts his wishes, he is much more likely to accept a decision that goes against those wishes.

It is within their reciprocal quality (i.e., each is talking and listening) that the conversations are effective in avoiding escalation and conflict while enhancing cooperation. For the conversation to be effective, however, it must truly be reciprocal. The parent cannot simply ask the child questions about his thoughts, feelings, or intentions without listening and being receptive to being influenced by the child's comments. If the child senses that what he says is not truly being heard, then this dialogue will most likely only further escalate tension. If parent's nonverbal expressions make it clear that her efforts are genuine, it is easier for the child to accept a failure to achieve consensus. Listening does not require agreement, but it does require the readiness and openness to be influenced by the statements of the other.

Conversations involving both talking and listening may be even more important for the development of the child's mind. As I discuss in Chapter 8, the child's reflective functioning includes the ability to be aware of his own thoughts, feelings, and intentions while at the same time being aware of the thoughts, feelings, and intentions of the other person. Thus he is able to be continuously aware of differing perspectives on the same object or event and is in a better position to choose the best possible response to the unique situation. He is able to demonstrate response flexibility.

With this skill, the child can begin to develop the habit of taking a mindful approach to situations to discover the best response, rather than simply reacting in an impulsive or compulsive manner. Stepping back to form his perspective, he can inhibit his first reaction, weigh the alternatives—including his parent's perspective—and respond in a more thoughtful manner. Reciprocal conversations facilitate such mindful approaches. They continue to occur within the child even when the parent is not present.

When the parent presents her perspective as the only one and issues a directive, she is doing little to foster her child's ability to develop meaningful, mindful decisions on his own in the future when she is not present. She is also reducing the child's readiness to consider the perspectives of others and the impact of his actions on others before making decisions.

Reciprocal conversations always integrate affective and reflective components. Within their lived presence in the person's life and relationships they are integrated within his experience. They roughly correspond to his emotions and thoughts, his nonverbal and verbal expressions. The reflective quality presents the general theme while the affective quality brings out how that theme is uniquely experienced in this situation with these individuals. The affective carries an immediacy to the communication about the experience whereas the reflective aspect brings a more detached perspective. Taken together, the affective and reflective enable the person to make sense of the experience and find its place within the person's life story. These components are considered separately in the next two chapters.

For a parent to facilitate these reciprocal conversations, she needs to feel safe herself. If she does not feel safe when her child questions her authority, she is likely to become angry and insist on compliance. If her child disagrees with aspects of her inner life, and she believes that only one perspective can be right so the other one must be wrong, she is likely to criticize her child's perspective. If interacting with her child reminds her of her own parents, or herself when she talked with her parents and was criticized for it, she is likely to react in a manner similar to how she and her parents reacted to each other years before.

As has been indicated, communication includes both verbal and nonverbal components. At times the nonverbal and verbal are not in accord. A child might say that he is pleased about something whereas his face might convey mild annoyance. He may express interest and willingness when his voice or breathing or gestures show that he is bored and impatient. When there is a discrepancy between the verbal and nonverbal, it is often wise to note it and be curious about it. By commenting—without judgment or criticism—that while he just agreed to do something his expressions seemed to suggest that he really did not want to do it, the parent is inviting the child to express his inner life more fully. She is showing interest in all of his thoughts and feelings, not just those that she might hope that he has. Such an invitation often leads to a cascade of words that might include the reasons why the child concealed his other wishes from his parent.

When commenting on the nonverbal, it is crucial to communicate acceptance of whatever the nonverbal represents. It reflects his inner life, which, hopefully, is not considered to be right or wrong. If the child is criticized for a look of annoyance, he is likely to become more secretive and less open to sharing himself with his parent. Much unnecessary and harmful parent-adolescent distance, in particular, is added to the adolescent's normal individuation tendencies because of such criticisms.

Conversation Tips

A parent may improve the reciprocal quality of conversations by keeping these tips in mind. She should:

1. express, at least implicitly, her underlying commitment to the relationship.
2. demonstrate that she is interested getting to know her total child, not just his behavior.
3. demonstrate—without lectures—that his reasons for his behavior are important, though they are not excuses.
4. convey her understanding of her child's inner life.
5. convey her enjoyment of and delight in her child.

6. discover her child's strengths or vulnerabilities that underlie his behavior.
7. demonstrate to the child that her intentions are to assist him in achieving his best interests.
8. convey empathy for her child's distress, including any distress caused by her discipline.
9. ensure that discipline will not jeopardize their patterns of open conversations.
10. demonstrate that conflicts regarding behavior do not jeopardize either her view of his worth or the relationship.
11. discover the best response to the given situation.
12. discover her unique child and reexperience her love for him.

Repairing Conversations

The following are ideas for making conversations more effective even when they begin with difficulty.

1. Stop the lecture. When noticing that she has been lecturing her child, the parent might pause, acknowledge it, change her tone, and invite her child's perspective on the event.
2. Take a break. When noticing that she or her child is experiencing a strong emotion that is making the conversation difficult, she might acknowledge the emotion and say that they both need to take a time-out and talk again when they are able to hear the other's perspective.
3. Say "I," not "you." When conversations regarding conflicts are difficult, the parent might practice giving "I-messages," focusing on behaviors and the parent's own reasons for being concerned. By "I-messages" I am suggesting that the parent begin the communication by saying clearly what she is thinking or feeling and the reason for it. For example:
   - I am angry when you tease our dog. I want her to receive the same respect that everyone else in the house receives.
   - I think that it is really important to help Grandma out this weekend rather than going to the shore. She won't ask, but I know she needs some help.

- I want to get the kitchen clean and shiny before we head out to the mall. If you want to help, we'll get there a little sooner. This will make her inner life more clear and give her child a chance to reflect on his own.

4. Practice curiosity. Recall the need to be curious without judgment. Practicing this habit is likely to be necessary for those who were not raised that way. Be curious about the thoughts, feelings, and behavior of the child, without judgment.

5. Rediscover the positive. When the parent notices that most of her recent conversations with her child involved conflicts and problems, she might focus on her child's interests and strengths and initiate discussions related to those or other positive themes.

Obstacles to Conversation

Certainly, some children, some of the time, are unwilling participants in conversations, even when they are reciprocal. Thus, a parent might see the value of such conversations but believe that they are not an option, because her child remains defensive, verbally aggressive, or noncommunicative when she tries to have a reciprocal conversation. She may be open about communicating acceptance, curiosity, and empathy but her child will not speak in a manner that enables her to do so. In the following example, a father wants to explore with his son why he stole from his sister, but his son is not willing to do so. The father might want to explore the aspects of his son's inner life that led to his stealing from his sister, but he is unwilling to discuss it. The father might then have believed that he had no choice but to punish his son, even if he does not know what might have led to his son's behavior.

Before giving up on this mode of communicating, the father might first reflect on whether or not he has used communication primarily for lectures and evaluations for a long time. If so, he might acknowledge that to his child, express understanding if those talks were difficult for him, and express his intention to communicate differently in the future. He might acknowledge that it will be new for both of them, so he hopes that they both can have patience with themselves and each other.

If that discussion does not create greater engagement with his child, he might focus on his child's unwillingness to communicate in spite of his assurance that he will not be criticized for what he thinks, feels, or wants. If he initiates this exploration with acceptance, curiosity, and empathy, the child might become engaged. For the child, talking about why he does not want to talk about stealing his sister's money might be easier than talking about stealing his sister's money itself.

Dad: Hey, Ted, help me understand why you stole your sister's money.

Ted: No!

Dad: Help me to understand, Ted. That's not something you've done before.

Ted: I don't want to talk about it!

Dad: You said that yesterday, so I thought I'd give us some time to think about it. I still can't figure it out. Could you help me?

Ted: No!

Dad: What's this about, Ted? How come you don't want to talk with me?

Ted: I just don't!

Dad: I can see that. What's it about?

Ted: I don't want to talk with you!

Dad: You don't seem to feel close to me at all now! Usually you've wanted to help me understand what's going on inside.

Ted: I don't now.

Dad: So are you really not feeling very close to me?

Ted: No I'm not!

Dad: I'm sorry about that, Ted. Even if we disagree, I like to be able to stay close . . . to talk about it and try to figure out our differences.

Ted: I don't want to!

Dad: Because . . .

Ted: Because you never listen to anything that I say!

Dad: Wow! No wonder you don't want to talk with me. It seems to you that I don't listen to you . . . so talking would be a waste of time if that's true.

Ted: It is a waste of time.

Dad: It doesn't seem to you that I listen to you. What makes it seem like that to you?

Ted: You never change your mind when we talk. You always are right!

Dad: So it seems like I never hear your point and change mine. Never!

Ted: If you would just listen to me I would not have stolen her money!

Dad: Oh, my, now I'm more confused. So the reason that you stole your sister's money has to do with your thinking that I don't listen to you. And that's why you don't want to talk with me . . . and that's why you're not feeling close to me . . . and don't want to be right now. There's a lot there, Ted. Help me understand.

Ted: But you won't listen anyway!

Dad: I'm trying. I really am! I want to understand but I don't. I do hear you saying that I don't listen, you don't want to talk with me, and because you see me as not listening, you stole money from your sister. Help me to put it together. I need your help.

Ted: I told you how important it was for me to go on the skiing trip! I told you but you said that I had to save half the money for it! And I didn't get half together.

Dad: And. . .

Ted: I really wanted to go and you let me down. So I stole from her to get the money that I needed!

Dad: Ah! You think that I wasn't listening or I would have come up with all the money for you. You thought that I hadn't heard how important it was for you to go.

Ted: Yeah, you just didn't listen . . . or you didn't care.

Dad: I'm sorry, Ted. I get it that you thought that was my reason for not giving you the money. That you just were not important enough to me to listen to you or care about your going. No wonder you don't want to talk with me if you think those were my reasons.

Ted: Well, what were they if I'm not right?

Dad: Since it was important to you, I thought that you would be willing and able to come up with your half. But you thought that I didn't really care if you went or not. That's probably why you didn't get your half. I was surprised that you didn't but now it makes sense. I'm sorry, son.

Ted: What are you sorry about?

Dad: I'm sorry that I was not more clear about my reasons. I'm sorry that I didn't show you that I could see how much it meant to you and was glad that you asked me for help to be able to go. I'm sorry that I didn't ask you about not getting your half. I'm sorry that I'm not as clear as I should be about how special you are to me. If I had been, you would have known my reasons and maybe talked to me about it.

Ted: Sometimes I'm not sure, Dad, what you really think of me.

Dad: I'm sorry about that, Ted. I really am. I'm going to make sure you know more clearly from now on. A lot more clearly.

After a conversation such as this, Ted would probably be much more receptive to talking about his stealing his sister's money and accepting responsibility for it. His dad, by keeping the focus on communicating their inner lives to each other, including their meaning to each other, was able to uncover a core issue under the stealing behavior. At the same time, the stealing was dealt with and Ted did not go skiing.

Attachment-Focused Dialogue

It was midafternoon on Saturday when Ann, age 6, and her dad came loudly into the kitchen from the backyard, where they had just spent 2 hours building snowmen and castles and horses. Both were cold, tired, and happy. Mom met them at the door, helped Ann to get out of her wet clothes, and listened to her animated tales of her adventures with her dad in the snow. As Mom prepared her a snack, Ann decided that she wanted to visit her friend, Susie, who lived a mile away.

As is often the case with children and especially younger children, the transition from an exciting event to one that is quieter tends to be emotionally difficult. They often become frantic in an effort to keep the excitement going. The experience of transition itself can often be disorganizing, causing a sense of freefall. During such transitions, the parent might best function as the parachute for a safe landing. Ann's demands reflect her agitated affective state and associated anger at her mother's response. Her mother communicates her desire to understand Ann's inner life by matching the affective state rather than talking in a very quiet or stern or annoyed manner. However, whereas Ann is agitated, her mother is animated.

Ann: I want to go see Susie now! I want to tell her what Dad and I did!

Mom: I'll bet you do! You had such fun! You can give her a call and tell her about it. It's too late today to go over and visit with her.

Ann: But I want to!

Mom: I know you do, honey. You can talk with her on the phone now and we'll talk later about visiting with her tomorrow.

Ann: No! No! I want to see her today!

Mom: Wow! I can tell! You really do.

Ann: Let me go today!

Mom: I can tell you want to see her, honey! I know you do.

Ann: Now! Take me to see her now!

Mom: Oh, honey, you really want to! And it must be so hard that I'm not going to take you today.

Ann: Now! Take me now!

Mom: So hard not to see her now! So hard that I said no!

Ann: Why can't I see her now?

Mom: It's too late, honey, and you've been so busy with your dad. Enough excitement and running around for today!

Ann: No! I want to see her!

Mom: I know you do, honey, I know!

Ann: Take me to see her!

Mom: Not tonight, honey. Not tonight.

Ann: Why won't you?

Mom: I told you already, honey. But you don't want to hear that, do you?

Ann: You're mean!

Mom: You are really mad at me now.

Ann: I am mad because you're so mean!

Mom: I know it seems that way to you, honey.

Ann: You are mean! You really are!

Mom: And you are really mad at me!

Ann: Why won't you take me?

Mom: Oh, honey. This is so hard for you! How can I help?

Ann: I don't want your help! Leave me alone!

Mom: But you're having such a hard time now! I'd like to help!

Ann: No you don't!

Mom: I do, honey! I do!

Ann: You don't like me!

Mom: Oh, honey, I'm sorry if it feels that way now.

Ann: You don't!

Mom: That must make it even harder for you if you think that I don't like you. So much harder!

Ann: I was having so much fun with Dad and you ruined it!

Mom: You were! So much fun with Dad. So much fun!

Ann: And now it's over!

Mom: And that makes it harder, doesn't it? The fun seems to be all over!

Ann: It is!

Mom: Would it help if we curled up under the blanket on the couch and I read you a story?

Ann: That won't help!

Mom: What would help, honey?

Ann: Nothing!

Mom: Nothing at all? How about if you pick out the story?

Ann: Can we read the one about the polar bear mom who found her lost cub?

Mom: If that's your choice, we can! I'm glad because I really like that one too.

Ann: I forget how the cub got lost.

Mom: Me too. I can't wait to find out.

Ann: Can we have some hot chocolate too while we read it?

Mom: I was hoping that you would ask! You and I think alike.

Ann: Well, you are my mom.

Mom: Well, you are my daughter.

Ann: Then we're alike.
Mom: And I'm glad.

Such conversations frequently lead to similar resolutions because of their reciprocal quality where there is a match affectively, joined awareness of the theme, and a joint purpose to communicate with each other, to understand and be understood. The parent needs to be focused on her child's inner life, join her there, and gradually invite her into a shared focus and activity. The child's original intent is to convince her mother to take her to her friend's house. After her mother refuses, her intent is to change her mother's mind. For Mom to be able to facilitate a shared intention, she needs to acknowledge her child's intention, express empathy over her distress about not achieving her goal, and lead her into accepting a joint intention that they can share, that is, giving and receiving comfort over her disappointment that she will not visit her friend that day.

Such dialogues are harder than they look because they are not characteristic of how many parents were raised themselves. But with practice and commitment, such conversations can become a reality in the relationship and can lead to fewer escalations and more resolutions of conflicts. This leads to much greater ease in facilitating repair following such conflicts. It leads to more successful transitions from one activity to the next during the course of the day. It leads to the development of both intimacy and autonomy, affective and reflective skills, and a flowering inner life along with many coping skills. Making such conversations a central feature of the parent-child relationship can truly bring the relationship to a new level.

CHAPTER SEVEN

Relate Emotionally

Children who are securely attached are much more likely to show healthy emotional development than are children who lack attachment security. Secure children are likely to have superior skills in the identification of emotional states within themselves and others, as well as in emotional regulation and communication. Children who experience habitual safety become very curious about and immersed in their world, and they experience it as fully as possible. Such active participation is certain to elicit a great depth and range of emotional responses to all sorts of events. The world of the child is so lacking if it does not ring with affective tones of varying rhythms and intensities.

Babies respond affectively, often in a sudden and intense manner, to many stimuli that are both internal (e.g., stomach pain) and external (e.g., loud noises or sudden movements). Similar intense affective responses occur during intersubjective experiences with their parents. They often appear to be very excited or deeply interested in these reciprocal interactions. When this affective response is intense, babies are not—on their own—able to consistently regulate the affective state so that it remains in a moderate range. Moderate affective experience enables the baby to maintain his interest and attention on an event while he explores it and discovers its qualities and nature.

The baby needs assistance from his parent to avoid moving into either a lack of affect or extreme, dysregulating affect.

When a parent is engaged with her infant intersubjectively, she is attuned with his affective state. He is able to stay with his mother's affective state and remain regulated—if she is—and engaged and attentive to the event associated with his affective expression. If he were alone, most likely he would not be able to regulate the affect that was emerging and he would become dysregulated. His behavior would become disorganized and he would lose his intentional focus on the experience. With his parent's active, matched, affective presence, he is much more likely to integrate his affective response to the situation into his overall experience rather than being overwhelmed by affect.

Sometimes babies are able to regulate their affective state by themselves. They do this by breaking the interaction that is causing the increased affect. Often, when babies are engaged with their parents intersubjectively, they take a break and look away. The attuned parent also takes a break and waits quietly until her baby is able to reengage. Sometimes the baby is not able to take a break from what is raising his affective state. Examples include bodily distress, noises or other external stimulation that he cannot turn off, or acute stimuli that frighten him. Even when a child might turn off the external stimulation, as by looking away from his parent, his emotional development might be more enhanced when his parent is able to expand his ability to stay in the interaction longer by coregulating the affect. This will encourage the development of his attention span and his ability to engage in intersubjective experiences.

Developing Emotional Competence

The following suggestions are good to bear in mind when parents wish to increase their child's emotional competence.

Remember Attunement

Affect attunement lies at the core of intersubjectivity, communication, and empathy and can also be seen as central in perceived safety, acceptance, and in how the parent's attachment history has an impact on her child. Affect attunement is crucial in the development of emotional competence. Without attunement, the infant and young child would have extreme difficulty learning to regulate their emotions and overall affective state. With regulation, the child is able to begin to identify emotions and express them in ways that are both understood and do not create relationship problems.

Emotional competence develops through countless interactions that involve the coregulation of affective states. When her child is animated, the parent is also is animated, and her child is less likely to become agitated. When her child is agitated, she remains animated, and her child becomes animated again. When her child is excited, she is interested and excited herself and her child does not become frantic. If her child is frantic, her energy is focused and confident and her child becomes excited again. When her child is calm, she is calm as well, and her child does not become listless. If her child is listless, she remains calm and engaged and her child becomes engaged again.

As the child's emotions become evident, the parent is able to remain attuned with each affective expression of his emotion, just as she was with his general affective state. When he is angry she is able to match the rhythm and intensity of the affective expression of anger, without becoming angry at her child for being angry. Her child is able to regulate his own background affect as well as the specific emotion of anger. When he is frightened, she is able to match his animated affective state without being frightened herself, and his fear then does not cause him to become dysregulated.

Michael: I don't like you! [with loud anger]
Mom: I hear you, Michael. You sound very angry with me right now! [matching the intensity and rhythm of his vocal expression]
Michael: I am mad at you!
Mom: You certainly are!
Michael: You won't let me play outside now!
Mom: No, I won't, Michael, and you really want to go outside!
Michael: I don't like you. [with a few tears and sadness]
Mom: And it's so hard now. Here, honey, let me give you a hug.

During this exchange, Michael's mother neither experienced nor expressed the emotion of anger toward her son, while she still matched the affective tone of his expression of anger. In so doing, his affective state—and his anger—became regulated and his anger decreased fairly quickly. If she had become angry, his anger would have escalated or he would have experienced the emotion of fear. If she had been quiet and rational, his anger would also probably increase, having to manage it on his own and not being able to regulate it.

The child develops an awareness of his specific emotional states, accepts them, and gradually comes to identify them with the words given to them by his parents. Securely attached children most often have parents who are able to accept all of their child's emotional experiences. These parents are as comfortable with their child's anger, fear, and sadness as they are with his excitement and joy.

Our emotions reflect the meaning of our ongoing involvement with all aspects of the world, both internal and external. We may experience delight when we see an old friend, excitement when we are successful at sports, worry when we face a challenge, sadness when our friend leaves on a trip. Other emotional experiences may be less obvious in their source but just as rich. We may experience joy when we see the mist rise from a lake, anger when we read about an event on the other side of the world, tranquility when we sit at home on a quiet afternoon with little to do, and satisfaction when we check off the last chore on our weekly list.

When a child is habitually dysregulated affectively, it is very likely that he will not be able to regulate any of his specific emotions. Not only will anger and fear become dysregulated easily, so too will excitement and joy. Other children manifest a generally regulated affective tone but become dysregulated around specific emotional experiences. In their development they may have routinely experienced attuned responses from their parents, but did not experience an attuned response to a specific emotion. For example, some parents may be very sensitive and accepting when their child is happy or sad, but become agitated and rejecting when their child is angry. In general, when a child's background affective state tends to be dysregulated often, his emotional development is more impaired than if his

affect regulation is habitually stable, while often becoming dysregulated when experiencing a specific emotion or two.

Say What You Really Mean

The emotional component of an interaction tends to be carried by
nonverbal features, while the verbal features carry more of the information being conveyed. When the words deny the emotions being expressed nonverbally, the child is often left unable to identify the
emotional states of others as well as his own. Accepting our own emotions and being unafraid to communicate them to others facilitates
our ease with them and their integration into the self. Emotions tend
to become poorly managed when they are not integrated with
thought and intentions and are not communicated coherently.

A parent may not want to communicate her emotion and so she
speaks very rationally. Yet her voice and face give her away and her
child knows that she is angry, which then activates his own reaction,
possibly made worse by his anxiety over what she might be concealing
about her thoughts and emotions. However, I am not suggesting that
the answer lies in speaking honestly with him about what you feel.
Such honesty, when the parent's thoughts and emotions are intense,
often leads to great emotional pain, hurts the relationship, and activates shame and anger in the child. A better response to such tough
honesty or to using a rational tone to hide an intense inner life is for the
parent to call for a time-out until she is calmer and can reflect on the
big picture better before giving expression to her inner life. At that
point, she can say what she thinks and feels without hurting or confusing her child. Better yet, if she needs to give herself such a time-out frequently, she would be wise to understand more fully what in her child's
behavior is activating such an intense response in herself, as well as,
what is making it hard to separate his behavior from his person.

Be Open to Your Child's Emotional Expressions

Securely attached children tend to have parents who are available,
sensitive, and responsive. Parental sensitivity involves an awareness

of the child's emotions and general affective state, and awareness is a guide to the best response to the child's behavior. When a parent recognizes and accepts her child's emotion—whatever it is—she is able to facilitate his emotional development, communication of his inner life, and his inner life itself.

Remember: An Attachment Relationship Is an Emotional Relationship

For an attachment relationship to provide safety for the child, it will necessarily be a relationship that is felt deeply, containing a strong affective and emotional component. An attachment relationship is associated with the emotions of love and anger, joy and sadness, safety and fear, excitement and grief, shame and guilt, sharing and jealousy. Attachment relationships are a fertile ground for the development of emotional competencies of significant depth and breadth. When the various emotions associated with the attachment are allowed the full range of expression, they become better defined and integrated, and they enable the attachment relationship itself to develop more deeply, fully, and with greater safety. If a child needs to inhibit all emotional expressions or the expression of specific emotions, the relationship will become more narrowly defined, less spontaneous, and more ambiguous. This would create the risk that the attachment itself would become less important to the child or that it will be less a source of safety for him.

In profound ways, emotions exist between two people in an intimate relationship as much as they exist within one person. When the emotional expressions associated with the relationship are welcomed and supported, the relationship itself becomes better defined, more spontaneous, and more satisfying. Along with greater openness to each other there is a greater sense of feeling understood by the other, as well as an enhanced sense of safety and a general openness to the world.

Developing Competence With Specific Emotions

If parents have had difficulty integrating a specific emotion into their own sense of what is acceptable to the self, their child may also have greater difficulty with that emotion. The greatest way for a parent to facilitate her child's emotional development is for her emotional abilities to have developed well. When that is the case, when a child shares his positive emotions with his accepting and engaged parent, they expand and become richer. When the same child shares his negative emotions, they become smaller and tend to dissipate. I wish to select three particular emotions now and describe their place in a child's development and in the parent-child relationship in more detail. Fear is not discussed now as it was explored in Chapter 2.

Anger

Anger often presents particular difficulties in one's overall emotional development as well as in the parent-child relationship. Many parents discourage, or even discipline, their child's anger when it is directed toward them (thinking it to be disrespectful) or toward a sibling (thinking that it was not indicated or might lead to a fight). When anger is indicated or appropriate will be considered in the next section on anger regulation and expression. Anger does not fit well with the "indoor voice" that parents want their child to maintain. Parents also often confuse the emotion of anger with angry behavior and are not able to help their child differentiate the two. Also, parents often isolate children when they are angry, for fear of reinforcing it, something that they would never consider doing for the emotions of sadness or fear. With such an attitude toward the child's anger, it is not surprising that the child often feels shame when he is angry, does not regulate it well, and has trouble remaining reflective while also being angry. Finally, he is not likely to learn how to express it appropriately and then repair any relationship problems that his expression of anger generates.

It is little wonder that such a child is often at risk to use anger inappropriately as a bully (too much anger; directs his anger inappropriately and at the wrong person) or as one who is bullied (too little anger; he becomes dysregulated by the anger of the other). It is also little wonder, when such children become parents and have children of their own, that they are at risk to use anger inappropriately when they discipline their own child.

Anger regulation and expression can be facilitated in the following ways.

Model Anger Regulation

The parent's own anger needs to be accepted and understood so that it can be regulated and expressed appropriately. She might try to revisit angry experiences from her own history in order to attempt to normalize the experience and differentiate her emotion of anger from any angry behaviors. If her child easily triggers her angry outbursts, she might explore the source of the trigger and reduce her child's ability to control this aspect of her emotional life. Parents are often correct when they say, "He acts that way just to make me angry!" When that is the case, the best way to reduce his acting that way is for her to control her anger. If she is emotionally strong and regulated, whatever the motives for wanting her to become angry (i.e., causing her to be upset since he thinks that she caused him to be upset; testing her readiness to follow through with a limit; testing to see if she is able to keep him safe), they will be less if she does not react with anger.

Express Anger Briefly

If a parent is angry at her child's behavior, she might express her anger quickly, focusing on the behavior, the reasons for her anger, and alternative behaviors for her child. She then might repair the relationship as soon as possible. This will require that she be in control of her anger so that it is brief and not directed at the child himself. Keeping the anger brief, to the point, and repairing the relationship quickly afterward will ensure that her child experiences her anger as being directed toward his behavior, not his person. It also will facilitate his ability to experience guilt over his behavior (when guilt is called for), rather than shame over his person (see Guilt and Shame below).

Match the Affect

By matching the nonverbal expression of affect when her child is angry—while staying regulated herself—she enables her child to remain regulated. (For example, "I don"t think you're fair!" causes her to reply, "I hear you, son. I know you think that!") This makes it less likely that the anger will escalate. She is communicating that she is able to accept, be curious about, and possibly experience empathy for the child's experience, while still being able to limit behavior that is associated with the emotion. After her child experiences her understanding of the intensity of his anger, he will be more likely to reduce his angry expressions when she begins to speak more quietly about his distress.

Accept the Child's Anger

The child will benefit when he can honestly express his anger toward his parent without it being evaluated. Often when children are not able to express their anger, they are likely to begin to limit the expression of other aspects of their inner lives. This often intensifies the common tendency of adolescents to conceal their thoughts, emotions, intentions, and beliefs from their parents. If a child cannot communicate his experience of a problem through showing that he is angry, he is likely to find behavioral ways to show his discontent. Parents certainly need to limit what words are acceptable for expressing anger, but hopefully some words will remain. The same needs to be said for nonverbal communications of anger through facial expressions and voice tone. It is wise to rethink the belief that when a child shows anger that he is being disrespectful. When children are given the right to express their anger directly to their parents, those children are likely to have a closer relationship with them, to accept their authority more easily and to less often show the anger through problem behaviors.

Accept Differences

While mutual understanding and agreement is certainly an important goal, often such an agreement does not occur. The child may continue to insist on his desire, not feel understood, and have difficulty accepting the parent's decision. In those situations, it is wise for the parent to completely accept her child's anger, though she might limit the manner in which it is expressed. Trying to reason her child out of his anger often only makes the situation worse. His anger does not represent a failure of the parent's discipline. It is often simply a natural expression of the frustration associated with the discipline. If the anger elicits anger in the parent, or doubt, or shame, the parent will try to rescue the child from his anger or suppress the anger. Emotional development is enhanced best if the parent simply matches the affective expression and shows understanding and acceptance, while still being clear and firm regarding the discipline.

Guilt and Shame

Shame and guilt are emotions that are given many meanings by professionals and parents, and so it is important that I clarify how they are used in this book. Although shame is often used interchangeably with guilt, I differentiate shame from guilt, following the theory and research presented by Tangney and Dearing (2002).

Shame precedes guilt in childhood development. It is directed toward the self, whereas guilt is directed toward behavior. With shame, the individual experiences the self as being bad, worthless, unlovable, or deficient in significant ways. With guilt, the individual experiences himself as having done something wrong—often causing pain or distress to another person—or failing to do something that he wanted to do. Given that shame is about the self, the person feels that there is little that he can do to fix it since he does not feel able to change the core of who he is. As a result, he is likely to deny what he did (e.g., lie), minimize it, make excuses for it, or blame someone else for it. When those efforts fail, he is likely to become enraged at the person who is making him focus on his shameful behavior. With guilt, the person is able to fix it since it is behavior that can change. If there were negative results that cannot be fixed, the person is often willing to accept or even seek a consequence for the purpose of restitution and relationship repair. With guilt, the person is focusing on the other and the effects of his behavior on the other. With shame, the person is focusing on the self and how to minimize the negative effects of his behavior on himself.

Individuals who are rated high on measures of shame are rated as low on measures of empathy for others, whereas individuals who experience guilt readily when they do something wrong are high on measures of empathy. Guilt, as defined here, is not associated with any measure of psychological problems, whereas shame is associated with many such measures. Excessive shame prevents the development of guilt, and when experienced in the present, it prevents a person from accepting responsibility for his actions. Regulating shame so that it remains limited enables guilt to develop.

Using this definition, when we speak about "too much guilt," we are actually referring to shame. When a person does something wrong to another, his guilt helps him to be aware of his effect upon the other and to motivate him to repair the relationship and to try not to do that behavior again. Then the guilt dissipates. Guilt signals that one's behavior has caused a problem to another that needs to be corrected. Its mission accomplished, it leaves. Shame, however, indicating a deficiency in the self that cannot be fixed, tends to stay, simmer, and express itself in many unhealthy ways (lies, blaming others, excuses, rage). Therefore, it is shame, not guilt, that I focus upon for the purpose of regulation. Shame regulation can be facilitated in the following ways.

Express Empathy

When a child expresses shame (e.g., I'm stupid, bad, selfish) it is not helpful to argue with him and say that he is not. Within the shame state, most children (and adults too) do not believe the other person. In fact, during states of shame, most children will attempt to hide from their parents in order not to be seen (as bad). The child is convinced that the other person either does not know him well, is lying, or must say that because of his place in his life (parent). When a child is expressing shame, experiencing and expressing empathy for him is often a much more helpful response. For example:

- It must be hard if you think you're bad.
- You really seem to be hard on yourself.
- That must be a very difficult feeling to have to carry around.

Such comments do not give the child anything to argue about and they help him to begin to feel understood. Such comments might lead to questions (curiosity) about when he started to experience himself as being bad, and if there are times when he does something wrong and does not experience it as a sign that he is bad. Later, when the child feels understood somewhat, he may ask—or the parent might tentatively comment—about her experience of him and whether it differs from his.

- Well, I don't experience you as being bad. I see you as making some mistakes at times, but not bad.

If the child is then receptive to hearing her experience of him, he may gradually begin to rethink his shame-based experience of himself.

Give the Child Time

When a child has done something wrong, he may react with anger and shame initially but with some time to calm down, he may be more able to address and accept responsibility for what he has done. He may react with shame when he feels trapped in a corner and anticipates intense rejection or criticism from his parent. When he feels safer, is calmer, and trusts his parent's response to what he has done, he may be able to address it and accept responsibility for it. He may actually feel safe enough to experience guilt, rather than shame. Insisting that a child defend himself, explain himself, or apologize immediately after he has done something wrong may make him more likely to react with shame, make the situation worse, and learn less from any discipline that is being tried.

Focus on Behavior

Since shame refers to the self and guilt refers to behavior, points that were made earlier about separating the self from behavior when disciplining the child are also helpful in facilitating guilt rather than shame. This involves not evaluating the child's motives for his behavior. It involves not assuming that we know his motives, because such assumptions almost always involve negative motives that will only elicit a defensive and probably shame-based reaction. The behavior needs to be addressed alone. Later, with curiosity and empathy, the inner life of the child that was connected with the behavior is able to be explored.

Repair the Relationship

Toddlers experience shame frequently when corrected by their parents for their behaviors, regardless of how sensitively the parents limit them. Such young children do not yet have the reflective capacity to regularly differentiate self from behavior, be aware of their parents' intentions, and perceive the effects of their behaviors on others. In such cases, to reduce and regulate shame, parents intuitively and wisely immediately repair the relationship with their toddler. They reattune with his affective state, provide him with comfort and support, and possibly redirect him into a modified or new activity. Such toddlers, safe in their relationship with their parents, often readily seek and receive comfort from the very person who caused their distress in the first place by saying no. With further development and with shame regulated, guilt becomes the primary socialization emotion to guide their behaviors.

Excitement

Excitement is an intense positive emotion that may be difficult to regulate and transition out of. Since it is a positive emotion, the fact that it may present problems for a child is often overlooked. The assumption is that the child will enjoy this emotion and the activity associated with it. "Too much of a good thing" is a phrase that can easily apply to excitement. Many vacations, special events, and surprises begin with laughter and reciprocal enjoyment and end with conflict and angry, hurt feelings. Parents initially feel proud that they are facilitating their child's enjoyment and end feeling confused and resentful that their child is never satisfied or doesn't appreciate what they have done for him.

Excitement regulation is as important as the regulation of anger or shame.

Parents will assist their child in regulating excitement when they participate in the activity with the child or at least be intersubjectively present in his experience. If a parent affectively matches the child's state of excitement, the child is more likely to remain regulated while in that state. If the parent is animated along with the child's animation, the child is less likely to become agitated and dysregulated. Joining the child affectively with voice tone, facial expressions, gestures, and movements is likely to help the child to experience the excitement along with the parent and enable him to borrow his parent's affect regulation abilities. If he is alone in excitement, he is more likely to find it escalating and be unable to regulate it. Then, as the activity winds down and the parent remains regulated as she transitions into a less stimulating activity, the child is much more likely to remain regulated as well. Even if the parent did not participate in the original activity, if she is affectively engaged with him—matching his animation— during the transition time into the quieter activity, he is more likely to make the transition successfully.

Parents need to recall and reflect upon their child's history to know how much excitement the child can regulate successfully. Parents might consider the nature of the activity, who else is involved, the length of the activity, the degree of stress or stimulation in recent activities, how tired the child is, and what is happening next in deciding how to organize the activity to regulate excitement.

If a child has habitual difficulty coping with excitement, the parent might review how much excitement the child is being exposed to. He may be habitually overstimulated. She might also discuss with the child the pattern of difficulty and explore possible coping skills. These might include accepting the need for his parent's guidance, direction, and limits during the period of excitement as well as engaging in his own self-regulation or self-soothing skills.

Obstacles to Emotional Competence

The following suggestions address two obstacles to the development of emotional competence.

Evaluating Emotions as Right or Wrong

Emotions are best understood as aspects of oneself, similar to thoughts, intentions, wishes, perceptions, and interests. As they are accepted, they can be understood, and their ability to guide our intentions and interests and to increase our insight into ourselves is increased. If a child is ashamed or afraid of his emotions, he will not understand their central place in his life. Rather he will focus on making them go away, or trying to change or hide them. Often, because of his resistance to their presence in his inner life, a particular emotion will only increase until he eventually becomes aware of what it represents in his life.

Emotions can be a valuable guide to

1. What is important to him
2. Whether something is in his best interest
3. Whether he is safe
4. The nature of his relationship with another person, including his perception of the inner life of that person
5. The nature of his own interests and values
6. What he needs to communicate about his own inner life

When we maintain an open acceptance of our emotions, seeing them as guides to understanding our inner lives rather than as something that is right or wrong, they are much easier to develop, identify, regulate, and express appropriately.

Emotions Function Best When Integrated With Thoughts

Emotional catharsis, which refers to the expression of an emotion simply for the sake of the expression itself, is of little, if any, value. As was just indicated, emotions are an excellent guide to aspects of our inner life. At the same time, our thoughts are also an excellent guide. Experienced and expressed together, thoughts and emotions are excellent means of communicating one's inner life. When either is expressed alone, the communication is limited and much remains ambiguous about the experience of the person, child or adult.

Children are often encouraged with the phrase "Use your words." This is valuable advice when the words represent the child's ability to reflect on his experience and connect it to specific words that enable his parent to better understand what it is. When a child is experiencing distress and can use words that communicate the nature of the distress, he will be able to elicit a helpful response much more successfully than if he had only screamed or cried.

At the same time, when a child "uses his words" but is told to do so in a flat tone, without any affective expression in his verbal communication, the parent will also be handicapped in her effort to understand the specific qualities of his distress. The affective tone of the verbal vocal expression goes a long way to help the parent understand the intensity, immediacy, and even the course of the distress. Such acts of using words tend to conceal more of the inner life than they reveal.

Sometimes parents regard the affective tone as a sign of disrespect and will command, "Don't you talk to me that way!" Regretfully, in placing limits on the expression of specific emotions or even his background affective state, the child is often less able to communicate the specific nature of his distress. He feels less understood by his parent, and, in fact, he is less understood. It might be wiser to limit the particular words that the child is using to convey his intense emotional state rather than trying to limit the nonverbal expression of the emotion itself. To give a child permission to tell a parent when he is angry, without giving him permission to express his anger with congruence between the verbal comment and nonverbal expression is likely to only generate miscommunication, deception, and avoidance of both forms of communication.

Attachment-Focused Dialogue

Sue, age 16, had asked her father if she could get her driver's license. When he said no, because she had not attained various goals that they had agreed she would attain prior to getting the license, she became very angry. In her anger, she called her father selfish, which caused him to dysregulate briefly and try to emotionally hurt her as she had just hurt him. There was an immediate risk that their anger would escalate and they would become objects of anger to each other. If that occurred, the intersubjective nature of their discussion would have ended and true communication would have stopped.

Sue: But everyone else is getting their license!

Dad: That's not my decision.

Sue: But maybe it should teach you something! You could be wrong, you know!

Dad: I'm doing my best!

Sue: Well, it's not good enough! You're just so selfish!

Dad: Now that's enough! It's fine to be mad at me but not fine to call me names.

Sue: But you are! You never think of anybody but youself!

Dad: That's rich! Look who's calling me selfish!

Sue: So you think I'm selfish? Thanks, Dad! Thanks a lot! That's just what I mean! You are selfish!

Dad: And who used that word first?

Sue: So what do you want me to say, "I did"? Ok, Dad, I Did! Are you happy now?

Dad: No! I'm not happy! . . . This is not getting anywhere. Please stop for a minute! Stop! We both have to stop!

Sue: Yeah, that's right! You win! Discussion is over!

Dad: No! [takes a deep breath, troubled look on his face as he stares at his daughter] I haven't won, Sue. I've lost. I've hurt you by suggesting that you are selfish. I haven't been the father that you need me to be. I'm sorry. You hurt me and I hurt you back. That's not the way for a father to treat his daughter.

Sue: How have I hurt you?

Dad: You're right, Sue! Let me say it better. I was hurt when you said that I was selfish. You were being honest with how you experience me right now. And I took it that you were hurting me, rather than just telling me your experience of me. So I tried to hurt you back. And I think I did. And for that I'm sorry.

Sue: Why'd you say it if you don't believe it?

Dad: I think because I try so hard to be a good dad. When you said that I'm selfish, I felt like I had failed to be a good dad. I failed you. And that hurt a lot. So I got angry with you for saying it and the way I expressed my anger was to try to hurt you back.

Sue: Thanks a lot!

Dad: And that's why I'm sorry, Sue. I'm sorry for trying to hurt you. And hurting you. I'm sorry that I forgot for a minute that I'm your dad . . . and that you're hurting now because I won't let you get your driver's license . . . and that you're trying to show me how important it is to you . . . and you're hoping that I'll change my mind.

Sue: It is important, Dad! It really is! Will you change your mind?

Dad: No, I won't, honey. I won't. But can we stay with what just happened for awhile longer?

Sue: What more do you want to say?

Dad: I want to know how you're doing now, after I suggested that I think you're selfish.

Sue: Are you sure you don't mean it?

Dad: No, I don't mean it. I know how much you do for your friends. And your little brother, and for the whole family. You give so much of yourself to others. No, I don't think that you're selfish.

Sue: Okay.

Dad: I think that you are pushing your beliefs at me strongly right now. I think that you're angry with me right now, and that your anger is part of why you think that I'm selfish right now. But I don't think that you're selfish.

Sue: Okay, Dad. I'm okay about it now.

Dad: Then help me understand about your calling me selfish. Are you saying that you think that my decision about the license has to do with my putting myself first and not considering you?

Sue: Well, it seems that way to me, Dad. It seems like you don't care how important this is to me and how much it hurts me that you won't let me get my license.

Dad: Okay, I think I understand more now. It seems to you that I'm selfish because it does not feel like I care that you're really disappointed now . . . that you want the license so badly. And yet I still won't let you get it.

Sue: Yeah, you think I'll just forget about it and be my happy self in 5 minutes. Or you want to think that so you don't have to notice how much this bothers me.

Dad: So it really feels like I'm letting you down. That you're not that important to me.

Sue: I know that I am, Dad. But it seems like you don't really listen to me when I tell you something is really important to me.

Dad: And I won't really listen because?

Sue: I don't know. You don't care? You're selfish? You don't notice me?

Dad: So no matter what you come up with, it hurts you because it says something about me to you, or about us, that we're not as close as you thought we were.

Sue: I guess not.

Dad: I'm sorry if that's how you make sense of this. That would make your not getting the license only a part of why this is so hard for you. You're also not getting confidence in our relationship . . . nor in who I am.

Sue: It's not that bad, Dad.

Dad: No?

Sue: No. It's just that I really want that license . . . and you said no. And I was mad at you, so I hurt you because it seemed that you were hurting me.

Dad: Do you think that was it? I hurt you by saying no, so you hurt me by calling me selfish, so I then hurt you by calling you selfish.

Sue: Yeah, I guess, and I'm sorry that I hurt you. I'm sorry that I called you selfish. You're really not. You are a good dad.

Dad: What changed your mind?

Sue: I didn't change my mind. I always think that you're a good dad. I just was mad.

Dad: Thanks, honey, for telling me that.

Sue: Anytime, Dad. Can I get my license now?

Dad: If I said yes, I don't think that I'd be acting like a good dad.

Sue: Yes, you would! [laughs] Okay, okay, I'll get working on my grades.

CHAPTER EIGHT

Reflect

Children are naturally and intensely interested in the world, both internal and external, that exists for them moment to moment. When they feel safe, the world that elicits and holds the interest of their parents and others strongly attracts them and becomes the organizing principle upon which they begin to create their own unique world.

The world of their parents is the psychological, cultural, and physical world. It is the parents' experience of the physical world—how they organize the physical world along psychological and cultural lines—that tends to most hold children's interest. It enables them to understand adults' behaviors. A child learns about that world through experiencing his parents' experience of it. How he navigates within the psychological and cultural world of his family and community will go far in determining his degree of satisfaction and competencies in his life ahead.

For the child to navigate the world of subjective experiences, he must develop skill at becoming aware of these experiences within both himself and others. He must be able to identify his emotional states, note their coming and going, and also influence their regulation. He must describe his perceptions and note if they differ from those of others. He must be aware of his thoughts about an event.

He must know what he intends to do and detect the intentions of others. He is both aware of his internal world and able to communicate its features to others. He can make quite good guesses about the internal worlds of others. Throughout this process, he is increasingly aware of the process itself. He is developing his reflective abilities, which are crucial in the development of his person.

The child's behavior increasingly becomes the tip of the iceberg. He is an active participant in both assimilating and accommodating to his world. His responses are both integrated and differentiated. He demonstrates flexible—neither rigid nor chaotic—interactions with the qualities of the environment which are both unique and common to other events and objects. His behaviors are the results of the active processes of his inner world in turn, through their influence on the world, further facilitate his inner-world development.

Without these reflective abilities, the child is left reacting to the world in an impulsive manner. With little organization, integration, and regulation of his emotional and cognitive skills, he reacts to many situations in similar repetitive or unpredictable ways rather than exploring and discovering the best flexible response for a given situation. His behavior is often ineffectual in dealing with the situation. Without reflection, he often does not learn from failure and thus is at risk to repeat the same maladaptive response the next time.

Addressing the behavior itself through external rewards or punishments often does not consider whether the child's inner world has sufficient clarity and organization to generate adaptive behaviors. Propping up behaviors rather than laying a proper inner-world foundation might manage a short-term problem without providing the child with the skills to manage all kinds of challenges and difficulties in the future.

Facilitating a child's reflective abilities involves providing him with a life rich in affective and reflective experience. This requires a model for reflective living, rather than teaching a specific cognitive ability. Noticing the inner life of oneself and others develops in children primarily through their engagement in intersubjective experiences with their parents and others. If he sees his parents experiencing his inner life negatively, he will also experience those qualities negatively and he will be less inclined to further explore those inner territories. If it seems that his parents have little interest in his inner life, he too will be much less interested in it. When his parents show interest in exploring and discovering his inner life, he will have the same open and curious attitude. More important still, he will discover that the process is not fixed. His parents will provide him with a process and a working model that becomes an invitation to continuously explore, organize, and reorganize a flexible sense of self and other. A lovely book by Myla and Jon Kabat-Zinn (1997) clearly describes the influence of the parent's reflective skills on those of the child.

Developing Reflective Skills

A parent can best facilitate her child's reflective skills in the following central ways.

Reflect Yourself

When a parent demonstrates an active interest in her own inner life, her child will notice and show a similar interest in his. When a parent's behaviors emerge from a coherent inner life, her child's behavior will tend to follow.

For example, Peter, age 7, and his father were driving through town when a car pulled out from a side street, requiring his dad to slow down.

Dad: You jerk!
Peter: What, Dad?
Dad: Oh, I just got annoyed with that driver for pulling out. He should have waited for me to pass.
Peter: Why'd he do that?
Dad: I don't know.
Peter: You called him a jerk. Is he?
Dad: Oh, I don't know, Peter. Maybe he had something else on his mind. Maybe he didn't think that I was going as fast as I was. I shouldn't have gotten annoyed with him. There was

no danger of an accident. He might be in a hurry for some
reason. Maybe it's important.

Peter: Why did you call him a jerk then, Dad?

Dad: Great question. I don't really know. Just a bad habit, I guess.

Peter: Sometimes you say that I should make doing something
a habit. Did you make getting mad at other drivers a habit?

Dad: Well, Peter, you got me there. Actually, my father often
used to get real annoyed at other drivers. Even when they
weren't doing much of anything. I think I just learned that
habit from watching him. I really never thought about it
much. I just found myself being like he was when I drove.

Peter: Do you think that I'll get the same habit from you, Dad?

Dad: I hope not. It takes some of the enjoyment out of driving.
I can be a safe driver without getting mad at other drivers.
I'll work at breaking my habit so you don't get it from me
like I got it from my dad.

Peter: Okay, Dad. Do you want me to help you?

Dad: You just did, Peter. You got me thinking about it.

Communicate Clearly

When a parent shows her intentions nonverbally and verbally, along
with associated thoughts and feelings, her child will have a more clear
understanding of the meaning of his parent's behavior. A parent who
is ambiguous about her thoughts, feelings, and intentions is generating anxiety rather than curiosity. With anxiety, her child is feeling less
safe and more focused on issues of safety than exploration.

For example: Mardy, age 11, was a bit bored and went searching
for her mother to see if she would be interested in playing a game.
She found her at her desk working with a calculator.

Mardy: Mom, how about a game of Mastermind? You able to
take a loss today?

Mom: Not now. Maybe later.

Mardy: Aw, Mom, Judy will be home from practice later and
I'll have other things to do then.

Mom: Not now, Mardy. I said maybe later!

Mardy: And I said Judy will be home later!

Mom: Enough! Now leave me alone!

Mardy: Geez! [She turns and leaves the room, annoyed and confused.]

Mom: [Shows a confused look as if she just became aware of what just happened between her and her daughter.] Mardy, come back for a minute, please!

Mardy: I got the picture! You're busy!

Mom: I am busy, but that's not what I want to say.

Mardy: What?

Mom: I want you to know I'm sorry for snapping at you. You just want to spend some time with me and I treat you like you did something awful. I'm sorry about that.

Mardy: That's okay, Mom.

Mom: I'm not pleased with how I just treated you. I'm kinda upset that my checkbook won't balance, which means that I don't have as much money as I thought I did. It's not that big a deal. It's just bothering me. And I took it out on you.

Mardy: So I wasn't just being a big pest?

Mom: No, sweetie, you were being my wonderful daughter who wanted to do something nice with her grouchy mom. And I grouched at you!

Mardy: And I still want to do something with you, grouchy or not.

Mom: I think that's a great idea. And it will give me a break from these numbers too.

Be Nonjudgmental

A nonjudgmental parent is able to perceive her child without needing her child to think or feel in a certain manner. This will enable her to discover what is unique about her child's inner life. In doing so, her child will be more able to perceive and reflect upon himself in a similar manner.

For example, Jimmy, age 8, saw his mother struggling with the groceries. He put down his video game and went to help her.

Mom: Thanks, Jimmy. I was having a hard time trying to carry all three bags.

Jim: I know, Mom.

Mom: I think that you wanted to help me.

Jim: Yeah.

Mom: I wonder why. Last month I think you would have just kept playing your game.

Jim: I don't know.

Mom: Yeah, and I didn't ask for help either. This might be one of the first times that you helped me when I didn't ask.

Jim: I guess.

Mom: I wonder why. Wait, do you think . . . why, Jimmy, I think that it's a sign of your getting older. You're growing up. Maybe not, but I think that's it! I think that might be the reason. What do you think?

Jim: I am getting older, Mom. I'm 8 now.

Mom: That's right . . . 8 . . . and getting bigger too, and stronger. I think that's it!

Separate the Child From the Behavior

A parent should differentiate her child's behavior from his inner life. While evaluating whether a behavior should be encouraged or discouraged, a parent might best convey acceptance, curiosity, and empathy, rather than judgment. The child will develop his reflective skills through having the freedom to be aware of his thoughts, feelings, and intentions. No aspects of his inner life are off limits.

Mary, a senior in high school, had recently gotten into trouble with her math teacher. She had yelled at him for something that she thought was unfair and now had to stay in detention after school for the rest of the week.

Mom: Hey, sweetie, what was that all about with Mr. Jennsen?

Mary: I really don't like him, Mom. I think he's a big jerk.

Mom: So that's why you yelled at him? What did you say anyway?

Mary: That he's a big jerk!

Mom: Ah! I see why you're in trouble.

Mary: But he is!

Mom: Well, honey, what you think about him is your business and your right. When you tell him what you think about him by calling him names, you are likely to get in trouble.

Mary: Even if they are true!

Mom: Yes, honey, even if they are true.

Mary: You always say that you will not criticize what I think.

Mom: Yes, I have said that and still do. It's how you communicate your thoughts that is the problem. You're not in trouble with your thoughts.

Mary: But he does act like a jerk.

Mom: If you had told him that you thought something that he did wasn't fair and you wanted to talk to him about it, I don't think you would be in trouble now. You took what he did, concluded that he was a jerk, and told him that. That's the problem. Name calling is not helpful. It does not solve the problem and makes the other person defensive and angry. My guess is that you would be angry if someone called you a jerk. It would not make you want to help solve the problem that the other person felt existed between the two of you.

Mary: But I'm not a jerk!

Mom: I don't think you are either, honey. Mr. Jennsen doesn't think that he's a jerk, either, I'm sure.

Mary: But he is.

Mom: And I think that you will be making a big mistake if you tell him that again when you think that he is. Think it if you want, but don't say it.

Mary: Okay, you've made your point.

Mom: I might make another while I'm at it. You might rethink your conclusion that he's a jerk because he did something that you disagree with. That thought—though it is your right to hold it—probably makes it harder for you to approach him to solve the problem.

Mary: How do I change my thought? It is what it is.

Mom: True. You might go slower about coming to the conclusion that he acts that way because he's a jerk. There might be other reasons. You might consider just telling him what you think is unfair about his actions and then be open to his reasons before deciding on them.

Mary: I guess you're right. Sort of like how you are with me.
Mom: Sort of. And thanks for that.

Accept Differences

When parents and their children become aware of and accept differences within their inner lives, they are the most secure and the inner lives of all will flourish. When differences are viewed as both acceptable and representative of healthy individuation, the reflective abilities of the child will be encouraged.

Kathy, age 16, told her father that she wanted to join a church that a good friend, Anne, attended. She and her family had been very active in her church all of her life.

Dad: So you are thinking of joining Anne's church. How come?
Kathy: I've gone a few times and like it a lot. They are really active in doing things for people who need help. Everyone seems to help out. They really seem to live what they teach in their church.
Dad: I think that we do too, honey. Maybe you're so used to what we do that you've taken it for granted.
Kathy: But they really do so many more things than our church does.
Dad: I think that church is more than helping others, Kathy. There are many programs that help others. Church is also about your beliefs in God and your beliefs in what God wants from us.
Kathy: Anne's church believes that we should all give 10% of everything we have to the church. I know that you don't give 10% of what you and Mom earn to your church.
Dad: You're right, Kathy. We don't. And our church does not set a minimum like that. We believe that everyone should decide in his own heart what he should give to God and the church.
Kathy: Then some people won't give and that's not fair to the others who do, and that's not what God wants.
Dad: How can you be so sure about what God wants, Kathy?

Kathy: I don't know, Dad. I just am. I think Anne's church is right about that.

Dad: Well, Kathy, I guess that we disagree on this. But I am glad that you are thinking about these things because they are really important in guiding your life, and you're going to be an adult who has to make many choices about right and wrong all the time. If you want to follow what you believe is right, I support you. I'll miss you in our church on Sunday, but I support you.

Kathy: Thanks, Dad. I knew you would.

About 6 months later, Kathy returned to her parents' church. Her beliefs were stronger than they were when she left.

Reflecting Upon Strengths and Vulnerabilities

When a child engages in behavior that his parents disprove of, and the parents negatively evaluate his motives, thoughts, and feelings along with the behavior, he is likely to develop a negative view of himself. The child comes to assume that his motives are negative. He often becomes convinced that he does possess the same negative motives that his parents perceive. The following are motives that parents may mistakenly attribute to their child's behaviors:

- He's just trying to get away with something.
- He just wants to make me mad.
- He doesn't care how it affects me.
- He just wants attention.
- He thinks that he knows everything.
- He's not trying.
- He's being selfish.
- He's being lazy.
- He's faking it.
- He just wants someone else to do it for him.
- He's jealous of his brother.
- He's scared to face the consequences.
- He thinks he's better than her.

- He's angry that I won't let him do what he wants.
- He wants to get it without having to work for it.
- He thinks that he doesn't have to keep his promise.
- He thinks that I won't remember what he's doing.

Even if the parent is right about one of these motives, her job is not done. If she goes deeper—finding the motive under that motive—she most likely will discover a motive that reflects a strength or vulnerability for which she can give support and empathy. Suppose the child seems to be not trying and the parent again asks why. She might discover that he is protecting himself from the pain of failure by not trying, which can easily be seen as a strength if he has no other ways to reduce that pain. Or his lack of effort may reflect his underlying sense of discouragement and hopelessness. She can certainly see that as a vulnerability that is easy to have empathy for.

It is important to remember again and again that when parents perceive a motive in their child, they are likely to be making that motive more prominent, even creating it when it was not present before they perceived it. If a parent is going to guess about her child's motives, she might be wise to find more positive motives since, in doing so, such motives are likely to increase. She might find motives that reflect strengths or vulnerabilities. In the former case, she is facilitating the development of these inner strengths, and in the latter, she is helping to regulate them through her empathy.

There may be many times when a child has a positive motive for a behavior that a parent disagrees with. If the parent is patient and does not assume a negative motive, she might discover that she agrees with his motive, though disagreeing with his choice of how to manage the situation. Here are some possible strengths or positive motives that a parent might perceive when her child misbehaves:

- You really seemed to want to help your brother.
- You showed great honesty in facing that.
- It took a lot of courage to bring that to me.
- I admire you for not giving up about that.
- You really want to get good at that.

- I can see you are really interested in that.
- Your friend is really important to you.
- Great job to control your anger when you were mad at me.
- I liked what you just did for your brother after upsetting him so much.
- I can see it bothers you when you hurt the dog.

At times, a child misbehaves because he has a major conflict about something or because choosing an alternative behavior might be very difficult for many reasons. Maybe he was in a vulnerable position and would never have chosen the behavior if it were not for these other circumstances. When a parent perceives a problem as reflecting an underlying vulnerability, the child is much more likely to be able to acknowledge it and address it. Most of us become somewhat defensive, if not angry, when another person identifies something about us as being a problem. We tend to experience shame since problems are often perceived as signs of deficiency, being wrong or inadequate. Being vulnerable, however, especially if we are able to rely on someone in those circumstances, is a normal part of life.

The following statements reflect states of vulnerability that a parent might perceive when a child misbehaves:

- It is so hard for you when you are not allowed to do that.
- You seemed so worried that he doesn't like you.
- You really are hard on yourself when you do something wrong.
- You seem to be so confused now about what happens.
- Nothing seems to be going right for you lately.
- It is so disappointing when you try so hard and it doesn't work out.
- It is so hard to find the right words.
- Sometimes you get so upset it seems to ruin your whole day.
- It seems to be hard to just relax and be confident that things will work out.
- You look so discouraged. I feel sad for you since you wanted that so much.
- You seem worried that I'll turn my back on you just because you made a mistake.

- When I got angry with what you did before, you seemed worried that I stopped caring for you.
- You look kind of lonely now that nothing that you hoped for is working out.

When a parent can find an associated strength or vulnerability in her child at the time of his misbehavior, the child is much more likely to accept the evaluation and limit on his behavior. In those circumstances, the behavior, not the person of the child, is being criticized. The child himself as well as the parent-child relationship are protected from conflict and negative judgment. The child is more able to face his misbehavior because he does not have to defend his motives, thoughts, and feelings. He is also free to be curious about the roots of the behavior. As he understands the thoughts, feelings, perceptions, and intentions that led to the behavior, he is in a good position to explore alternative behaviors in the future that might better address those qualities of his inner life that his behavior attempted to rectify. Also, being able to differentiate his inner life from his behavior, he is more able to experience guilt, when appropriate, and not shame.

Attachment-Focused Dialogue

Nine-year-old Nathan will not come to dinner after being corrected by his father for not helping his 6-year-old brother, Ed, get his bike out of the garage before he went riding himself. His mother was not aware of the problem until her husband told her that Nathan was refusing to come for dinner.

Mom: So what's going on?
Dad: He's in his room pouting because I got angry with him for leaving Ed behind and riding his bike without helping Ed get his bike out.
Mom: What did you say to him?
Dad: I just said that since he didn't do what I told him to do, he couldn't ride his bike.
Mom: And what did he say?

Dad: He said that I wasn't fair since he tried to get Ed's bike out and he couldn't do it.

Mom: And you said?

Dad: That if that was true, he should have come and told me instead of just leaving.

Mom: And he said?

Dad: He said, "I told Ed to tell you," which was his way of not accepting responsibility for his actions. He just wanted to get away with something.

Mom: And you told him that.

Dad: Yeah, I said that he just wanted his own way and he needed to face it when he does something wrong.

Mom: Why don't I go upstairs and talk with him? [She leaves the kitchen.]

Mom: [after knocking on her son's bedroom door and entering] Hey, Nathan, I hear that you and your dad had a conflict. How you doing?

Nate: He never believes me!

Mom: Ah! Sounds like you're not doing very well. Seems to you that your dad does not believe what you tell him.

Nate: He doesn't! He just thinks that I'm lazy and do whatever I want! He thinks that I'm just being selfish all the time!

Mom: Oh, Nate! No wonder you're having a hard time. No wonder, if it seems to you that your dad thinks that you're lazy and selfish. No wonder you're upset over what happened between you two.

Nate: He doesn't like me, Mom! He doesn't!

Mom: Oh Nate. You think that your dad doesn't even like you!

Nate: He doesn't, Mom. [tearful]

Mom: What makes you so sure?

Nate: He says that I didn't do what he told me to do because I'm lazy and selfish!

Mom: Did he use those words, Nate—lazy and selfish?

Nate: No, Mom, he said that I was just trying to get away with something, but that's the same thing. That's what he meant.

Mom: So you say that your dad made a mistake about why you didn't tell him that you couldn't get the bike for Ed. What do you think was the reason, Nate?

Nate: I don't know. But I wasn't being lazy!

Mom: I hear you, and I don't believe that you were lazy either. Though I'm not sure that your dad thought that you were lazy when he said that you were trying to get away with something. But I'm still curious about why you didn't tell your dad that you couldn't do it.

Nate: I told Ed to tell him!

Mom: Because.

Nate: I don't know!

Mom: What did you think would have happened if Ed told your dad?

Nate: He would have come out and got Ed's bike out of the garage.

Mom: And then what did you think would happen?

Nate: I don't know.

Mom: Did you think that he would have said anything to you?

Nate: [Suddenly looking very sad and becoming tearful again] I thought that he would see me riding and I'd yell and he'd watch me do a new trick in the driveway that I've been practicing.

Mom: Ah! You hoped that he would see how well you can ride your bike.

Nate: He never watches me ride my bike! He doesn't know how good I am riding it.

Mom: And that seems like it would be very special to you, that your dad would be proud of how well you can ride now.

Nate: Yeah, I just wanted him to tell me that I'm doing really well now riding my bike.

Mom: And instead, it seems that your dad is disappointed in you for not doing what he told you to do. Rather than being proud of you, he's disappointed in you! Oh, my, Nate. No wonder this is so hard for you. You were hoping to be closer to your dad and instead it seems that you two are further apart.

Nate: How come, Mom? What did I do wrong?

Mom: What do you think?

Nate: Not coming and telling him that I couldn't get Ed's bike.

Mom: Yeah, I can see that might have helped. And maybe your dad might have handled it differently too. Maybe he could have asked you why you didn't come and tell him yourself, rather than assume that you were just trying to get away with something. Maybe if he knew that you were hoping he would come outside and see that new trick with your bike, he would have understood and not become angry about your telling Ed to tell him.

Nate: Do you think so, Mom?

Mom: I'm not sure, Nate, but I do know that your dad loves you a lot. I know that your reason for telling Ed to get your dad makes sense to me and most likely would make sense to your dad too. And I think that if we told him what we just figured out, he would want to know and he would feel very sad that you think that he thinks you're lazy and selfish. I think he would want to talk with you, Nate, and work it out and be close to you again.

Nate: Do you think so, mom?

Mom: Yes, I do. Should I send him up to talk with you a bit before you two eat?

Nate: I guess.

Mom: Good. And maybe there will be time for both of us to see your new bike trick before it gets dark.

Mom: (Leaves Nate's room and returns to the kitchen.) Honey, would you go up and talk with Nate for a little bit? The meal can wait.

Dad: Sure. What's up?

Mom: Well, I think that he's worried now about what you think of him.

Dad: Well, I am upset that he didn't do what I said and then didn't face it.

Mom: Do you know why he didn't do what you said?

Dad: He just took the easy way so he could ride his bike without thinking of Ed.

Mom: That's a fair guess, but I think that you might have listened to him tell you why he sent Ed in rather than telling you himself.

Dad: Is that important?

Mom: I think it's really important. I think that knowing why he did it would help him feel that you don't dislike him if you still disagree with how he handled the situation.

Dad: Dislike him?

Mom: Yeah, honey. When you guessed why, you guessed a motive—to get to ride his bike without worrying about his brother—without really knowing if that was his motive. We talked a bit, and he told me that he had another motive that is not selfish in any way. I think that if you knew what it was, you might not have been so annoyed with him for not telling you about Ed's bike.

Dad: So I messed up?

Mom: Just like I do at times and you bail me out. I think that you judged his motives without checking it out with him, and your guess made you more upset about his behavior. So if you're just curious about his motive, I think that you two will work it out.

Dad: We've been over this before, haven't we?

Mom: How we guess our kids' motives, yeah, a lot, for both of us. Let's not be too hard on ourselves. I can't recall my parents ever wondering, without anger, about my reasons for doing things. So we're doing better. And when we make a mistake and fix it, I think that Nate forgives us and knows that we really do love him and don't judge him. We're getting it right. Slowly, maybe.

Dad: Okay. I'm off. Keep our dinner warm.

CHAPTER NINE

Repair

Healthy relationships have conflicts. Healthy relationships have periods of separation, misunderstandings, and differing interests and priorities for how to spend time in the present. And when the relationships involve parents and children, healthy relationships involve discipline.

Parents are definitely not continuously and accurately available, sensitive, and responsive to their infants. Very frequently they misread their infant's expressions of what he wants. Often they have other responsibilities, and their delayed response or failure to respond to their infant's desires causes frustration and even distress for him. Or the infant may want something and the parent does not respond quickly, believing the infant will not suffer from—and may even benefit from—the experience of periodic frustration. In all of these cases, the infant's attachment security is not hindered because the parent consistently repairs the relationship after the separation, mistake, delay, or lack of response. The parent returns and is again available, sensitive, and responsive. The parent acknowledges the child's distress by matching his affect, and then comforts him. The relationship actually deepens as the child knows that in spite of separations or differences the relationship always continues. The child also learns that while his parent may not always respond to his wants, she will always respond to his needs. Relationship repair is a crucial and central part of security achieved in an attachment relationship.

Without ongoing repair of a relationship, whether it is between parent and child, partners, good friends, or family members, the relationship will either end or move into a more distant and lighter mode in which one individual does not rely on the other as an attachment figure. Or one may rely on the other in selected areas but not in those that have not led to a beneficial response or repair in the past.

Developing Relationship Repair

Maintaining the balance between the wishes and interests of the individual and what appears to be best for the other members of the family is a necessary reality in every home. Without the unique features of each individual's inner life, the family would resemble a bee colony. Without the family's joint interests and intentions, each individual would be solitary and would focus primarily on his own interests. Without shared affect, awareness, and intentions (intersubjectivity), members of the family are likely to be lonely individuals. Without conflicts, separations, misunderstandings, and discipline—as well as the repair required by these realities—family members would lack individuality.

A hurdle for many families is knowing what to do after there has been a break in the relationships between members of the family. Such breaks, in the context of a lack of felt safety in attachment, tend to create emotional arousal that may be difficult to manage. Knowing that, many parents and children tend to avoid possible breaks by trying to overlook them or through compliance or permissiveness. When breaks do occur within families who are not comfortable with them, one of two reactions tends to result. First, the emotion generated by the break may lead to intense anger, fear, sadness, or shame. Any of these emotional states only magnify the original break and cause a risk of escalation that will make the break even more difficult to repair. Second, the emotional response may be avoided and denied so that the break doesn't matter. Such a short-term means of avoiding a negative emotional state moves the relationship toward a less intimate and meaningful place. By claiming that the break does not matter, the likelihood is that the relationship itself will matter less.

Breaks Caused by Separations

Throughout childhood, there will be many times when a child is separated from his parents for minutes, hours, days, or even weeks, months, or years. These separations are likely to create varying degrees of distress in the child. The younger the child, the shorter the periods of separation that will to create distress. What is crucial to remember as parents is that there is no objective degree of distress that is appropriate for a child at a given age. There is never reason for a parent to respond to her child with laughter, anger, or indifference because he is acting "like a baby." At the same time, when a child manifests a high level of distress, a parent does not have to conclude that the separation was too much for the child to manage and therefore needs to be stopped.

A child's distress needs to be accepted as it is. He is communicating that the separation has left him feeling anxious and unhappy. He is expressing his subjective experience of the separation. Explaining to him that his distress is unreasonable is probably not going to reduce it. Being angry or ridiculing a child is either going to increase his manifested distress or cause him to conceal it. Such reactions will not decrease the experience of distress.

Dismissing a child's distress is likely to increase it. However, if the parent takes the opposite approach by trying to eliminate distress through avoiding separations, she is also likely to increase it. When a parent tries to prevent her child from having any distress when there is a separation, she is communicating that he cannot manage the distress. She is communicating that distress is bad and should be avoided at all costs. In so doing, she is showing a lack of confidence in her child. Because he lacks confidence, she does too. Her reactions show that he does not have the emotional strength to manage the distress associated with separations.

While accepting the child's distress, the parent is wise to also try to understand it better. This requires a nonjudgmental attitude of curiosity in which she is clearly making the effort to enable the child to describe his distress in greater detail. As he begins to express the distress, his parent's response of empathy will help him feel support and comfort and that he is not alone. Even if the separations do not change, the child is more likely to feel less alone. His parent is psychologically more present for him even though they are physically separated. The distress itself, being carried in part by the parent, is less.

It is this middle way that enables the child to manage distress and become stronger through periods of routine relationship breaks due to separations. The parent neither rejects her child's distress nor rescues him from it. She acknowledges it, experiences empathy with him over it, and so helps him to contain and reduce it. At the same time, she understands that separations are difficult for him. She does not dismiss that. She explores ways to help her child to cope more successfully with the distress—without rescuing him.

Parents still need to be sensitive to the fact that frequent separations may undermine a child's sense of safety. Frequent unnecessary separations are likely to be experienced by the child as a sign that being together is not that important to his parents. It may seem that they have more important priorities. Since being with his parents is a very high priority for him, he may be confused because he does not experience a similar desire from his parents toward him. He may begin to believe that he is somehow failing his parents because he is not that special to them.

To reduce their child's fears, his parents would be wise to share the reasons why the separations are required. They might be willing—when possible—to reduce the separations. They might share their own sadness that they are not able to spend as much time with their child as they would like.

Often in contemporary life, both parents are employed outside the home and have various other responsibilities that take them away. Along with natural desires to pursue interests and time together without children, quite a number of routine separations occur that are often overlooked. Their child's distress may also be overlooked, and eventually the child stops showing distress. This may not indicate that he experiences safety and accepts the separations. It may rather suggest resignation, and possibly place the child at risk of developing patterns of misbehavior in an effort to force a decrease in his parents' absence. The child may also develop an overreliance on self and peers that indicates that his parents are less important to him than he needs them to be and they would like to be. This creates some of the accelerated independent wishes of adolescence that can generate many parent-child conflicts.

The following are some ways to assist a child in dealing with separations from his attachment figures:

1. According to the child's ability to understand, provide information regarding the circumstances of the separation, its length, purpose, and where the parent will be.

2. Accept any expressed emotions regarding the separation. Encourage their expression with matched affect, empathy, and curiosity.

3. Provide concrete indicators as to when the separation will end, whether it be hours (marked on the clock, with an alarm, or by clarifying that it will end following a specific daily activity) or days and weeks (marked on the calendar, related to a day of the week or planned activity).

4. Provide the child with regular, predictable phone check-ins in which there is an exchange of information about their activities and in which the importance of the relationship to the parent is apparent to the child.

5. Provide the child with specific reminders of his parent throughout the day and week. These may be concrete objects or remembered joint interests.

6. Have the parent loan the child something of hers to keep nearby until her return. Similarly, have the child loan the parent something of his.

7. Have an activity associated with mutual fun planned for when they reunite.

8. Invite the child to sleep with an article of his parent's clothing that smells like her.

9. The parent should express to her child that she misses him the same way he misses her. She may have to be separated, and she is sad about it because of her relationship with her child.

10. The parent is clear that she looks for ways to reduce the duration or frequency of separations when possible.

Billy, age 6, manifested angry crying outbursts and difficulty sleeping
over the past week, seemingly because his father had not been home
for dinner 3 to 4 nights a week for the past month. A number of problems had emerged for his dad recently, in his work as well as with his
mother, whom he needed to help out temporarily in the evenings.

Dad: You seem to be having a hard time lately, Billy. What do
    you think it's about?
Billy: I don't know.
Dad: You don't? Any guesses?
Billy: No.
Dad: I was wondering if maybe . . . it's because I'm not home
    much in the evenings. We don't get to eat dinner together
    much and I can't put you to bed either.
Billy: No, you don't! Why?
Dad: Good question, Billy. I'm not home and you want to
    know Why.
Billy: Yeah, why don't you come home anymore?
Dad: Sometimes I have to stay late at work and sometimes I
    have to stop by Granny's house and take care of her for
    awhile. I wish that I didn't!
Billy: Why do you have to?
Dad: Well, there is a lot of extra work this month, and the
    person who helps your Grandma in the evening is in Florida
    for a month, and Grandma needs some help.
Billy: Why?
Dad: Lots of questions! I think that you might want to
    say: I don't care about work or Granny. I want you
    home, Dad!
Billy: I do want you to come home!
Dad: I knew you did, Billy! I knew it! And I want to come
    home too.
Billy: Why don't you?
Dad: I want to! I really do want to.
Billy: Do it then!

Dad: I want to do it, but Grandma can't take care of herself very well anymore and she needs my help, Billy.

Billy: I need you too, Daddy.

Dad: Oh, Billy, I know that you want me to come home. A real lot! I want to come home and see you and play with you and put you to bed. I Really do! But I need to be with your Grandma some nights now.

Billy: I miss you, Daddy.

Dad: And I miss you, Billy. I really do. I miss you so much.

Billy: When will you stop being late, Daddy?

Dad: Two more weeks. Twelve more days. And I can't wait!

Billy: I can't wait either.

Dad: I have an idea to help us both wait. How about, when I'm not home, if you draw me a little picture and leave it for me on the table so I can see it when I get home. And I'll draw a little picture for you to look at when you wake up in the morning.

Billy: Okay, Daddy. I'll draw a picture for you.

Dad: And I'll draw a picture for you too, Billy.

Breaks Caused by Discipline

Acts of discipline frequently create a break in the attachment relationship, no matter how short and mild. When the child's intention is not matched by his parent's intention, there is a lack of intersubjective experience. Parent and child are not insync. A very young child is often quite distressed by this, having difficulty comprehending why his parents would not want to share the same experience with him, or at least actively enjoy what he is choosing to do.

With a toddler, it is easy to see how his relationship with his parents is the source of deep joy and absorption as well as frustration and distress. Moments of intersubjective sharing often create magic; moments of discipline often create despair. When parents say no, the toddler often experiences shame, seeing his parents as turning away from him and not being responsive. The toddler feels that he has somehow let his parents down, while also feeling that they have let him down.

In situations characterized by attachment security, this profound effect is resolved quickly by both the parent and toddler. Parents provide comfort to assist the toddler in managing the negative affects of shame and fear, and toddlers often go to their parents immediately for comforting. Even though it was the parent's word that caused the distress, the toddler nevertheless turns to the same parent for comfort. Even though the toddler may have done something that needed to be limited, parents intuitively tend to give comfort to their toddler without worrying that they will reinforce the behavior or spoil him. Parents need to continue to trust their intuition.

Through the act of comfort following the act of discipline, the parent and toddler both experience that the person and the relationship are more important than any action that either of them has taken. They had a disagreement about the merits of the toddler's action, but the need for safety and reestablishing closeness in their relationship is not forgotten.

Parents may err by attempting to help their child avoid distress by allowing him to do what he wants to do. Most are aware that being permissive will only cause greater behavioral problems in the future, and so they work to follow through with their directives. Or they may err in not noticing or helping him to manage his distress when he is limited. When that occurs, the child is receiving the message that his behavior is more important than his inner life. Or they may err by not allowing him to express his distress and annoyance. In that case he is receiving the message that his inner life is also being evaluated and it is not allowed to contain any negative emotion directed toward the parents. Not only does he have to change certain behaviors to conform with his parents' wishes, he also has to either change his inner life or conceal it from them. Either course of action is placing his emotional development and his relationship with his parents at some risk for difficulties in the future.

Again, it is important to stress that discipline functions to teach, guide, or direct a child's behavior. Being clear about the reasons for the limit or consequence helps the child to sense that the discipline is motivated by the parent's perception that it is in his best interests. When it is given with empathy rather than anger or the threat of relationship withdrawal, the affect associated with it remains regulated and the child is able to reflect on it, often reluctantly seeing the parent's perspective.

A helpful analogy is to think that discipline involves two hands. One hand focuses on the child's behavior and the need for limits, or redirection, or alternatives. The second hand focuses on the inner life of the child, with acceptance, curiosity, and empathy over both the factors that led to the behavior and the possible distress caused by the limitation. If a parent can nurture her child's inner life while limiting his behavior, he is likely to much more readily accept his parent's direction and understand the reasons for the discipline, while feeling safe in the relationship and in his self-worth.

Breaks Caused by Parental Mistakes and Misattunement

Given that parents are not perfect, it is wise for them not to pretend that they are. Parents might well acknowledge to their child that their behavior is less than parental at times. Since parents value having their children acknowledge their mistakes, it is helpful to model for their children that they make mistakes too. When they accept responsibility for their mistakes, they are reassuring their child that he is not the only one who makes mistakes. When they apologize to their child, they are asking for forgiveness, a request that helps him feel valued. He sees that while he may be a child, he still deserves the same quality of treatment that his parents ask from him. By apologizing for their mistakes, parents are also showing that they are committed to preventing or reducing mistakes because they take their parenting responsibilities very seriously.

Of course, telling their child that they are sorry is not sufficient if they are not also taking steps to reduce their mistakes and to prevent serious mistakes from happening at all. If a parent screams and swears at her child, her commitment to his safety needs to be such that she will do whatever she needs to do to ensure that it will not happen again. She cannot blame her swearing on his behavior, nor on her partner, nor the stresses of life. As she realizes that her rage is harming her child's development as well as their relationship, she must prevent its recurrence. She may benefit from seeking help from a professional who specializes in parenting, parent-child relationships, or assisting her with her own attachment history.

*Breaks Caused by Parents Having Other Responsibilities
and Interests*

For the infant and toddler, in fundamental ways, his parents are experienced as an extension of himself. With intersubjectivity, he has some awareness that he cannot control his parent in the same manner that he can control his hands, but he still has such success in eliciting a contingent response from his parents that he experiences a connection with them that is safe and certain.

As the weeks go on, the toddler has an increasing awareness that his parents do not always respond as he wishes and in fact are now responding less to his wishes than they did in previous months. His parents seem to have a life that is at times separate from his. While present—unlike the times when they disappear during separations—they are nonetheless not responsive. The toddler is likely to be puzzled by this development. Does this mean that his safety is compromised? What he experiences as a need does not elicit a contingent response from his parents. Are they no longer willing or able to meet his needs? Is he now less safe?

The toddler is learning to differentiate his needs from his wants. His parents always respond to his needs, but there are many times when they do not respond to his wants. If they fail to respond to his needs, his safety is indeed jeopardized. He might become ill from lack of food or shelter; he might become injured through lack of supervision; or his psychological development might be compromised through lack of engagement. However, if they fail to respond to his wants, he remains safe, though possibly frustrated, disappointed, or annoyed.

If the child cannot understand his parents' separation of wants from needs, their failure to respond to his wants is likely to produce confusion and a loss of the sense of safety. It is clearly in his best interests to be able to understand what is in his parent's mind when she does not respond.

When a parent fails to respond because of other responsibilities or interests, she has caused her child distress through both the immediate frustration of an unmet desire and also the perceived break in the relationship. To repair the relationship at that moment is an important step in assisting a child to understand the difference between wants and needs. Repair is facilitated by:

1. Noticing the child's distress and expressing understanding and empathy for it.
2. Giving a brief account of her reason for not responding to his desire.
3. Communicating (nonverbally more than verbally) her confidence that her child will manage his distress and that he remains safe.
4. Offering a coping skill (i.e., waiting, choosing another activity, seeking a hug) to assist him in managing his distress.

Often, simple acknowledgment, empathy, and suggestions suffice for the child to manage distress and continue with his own pursuits while his parent is pursuing hers. At times the child will make a stronger case that he does not want to wait and that his distress is larger than his parent thinks. Most often, there is no need for a repeat of steps 2, 3, and 4; rather, a simple empathic phrase will suffice to enable the child to accept his parent's decision. The child will develop greater frustration tolerance when his parent has empathy for him and confidence that he will accept the situation.

It is crucial that a parent does not believe that she is responsible for eliminating distress in her child's life. Distress—successfully managed—is a necessary part of child development. Distress associated with unmet wishes, not unmet needs, will facilitate the development of a child's coping skills. Her confidence will lead to his own confidence that he can manage distress in the future. This awareness is an important component of resiliency. This is not to suggest that a parent should deliberately create distress for her child. Distress happens often enough on its own.

The parental attitude that will best help a child to manage distress and facilitate repair involves empathy. It is not wise to deny distress or to reason a child out of it. Nor is it wise to let him manage it alone. Rather, acknowledging, understanding, accepting, and having empathy for it will enable a child to learn that it is not too much to handle, that his wishes are of value—though at times not met—and that he remains safe and important to his parent even when she does not respond as he wishes.

After the break, there is value in simply being together and briefly enjoying the repair itself. During the break, one or both were likely to experience some defensiveness, isolation, or anger. They were likely to be somewhat tense and vigilant. When there is repair, it is helpful for both to experience the relaxation and enjoyment that comes from safety and closeness in the relationship again. During the repair, the child is likely to soften and allow himself to be comforted by his parent. The parent is likely to soften and want to comfort her child.

Repair of the relationship when there has been a break completes the circle. It reassures the child that breaks are natural occurrences and will not destroy the relationship. Breaks need not be feared nor avoided when they naturally occur. Breaks remind both parent and child that the relationship is important to them—more important than the circumstances that created the break. By accepting and addressing them, they remain small. By fearing or avoiding them, they become larger. By failing to repair them, they can undermine the safety needed to make attachment a steadying force in the developmental trajectory.

Obstacles to Repair

Believing that repair is not that important is the central obstacle to relationship repair. This assumption tends to be based on three reasons:

1. The belief that the distress of the break will gradually fade away.
2. The belief that the parent is weak if she initiates repair when the child's behavior caused the break in the first place.
3. The belief that if the parent initiates repair, she will be reinforcing misbehavior.

Let us look more carefully at those three assumptions.

First, it may well be true that over time the distress caused by a break in the relationship will lighten. When both parent and child gradually relate to each other as if nothing happened, the child certainly will feel some relief that the break has ended. However, one risk is that some ambiguity may remain as to whether the relationship was weakened by the break. This uncertainty is likely to place attachment security at some risk. The child may wonder whether the break affected or reflected his parents' views about who he is. Doubts may even emerge as to how important the parent-child relationship is to the parent.

Also, without resolution of the break—which repair would facilitate—there is a likelihood that the issues will emerge again and again and a maladaptive relationship pattern may result. Eventually the factors that caused the break are seen as always occurring or never prevented. With repetition, both parent and child are likely to experience the break as something that represents their relationship, not an isolated event or disagreement. They begin to think that the other doesn't care or isn't trying to improve the relationship. In contrast, when the break is repaired, the importance of the relationship is affirmed. The event is treated as a single event, and if similar issues arise in the future, both tend to be confident that it will be managed. When subsequent similar breaks occur, the repair of the relationship is much easier.

Second, initiating repair does not imply that the parent is weak. Rather, such initiation indicates clearly that the relationship was very important to the parent, and regardless of the nature of the break, it is still very important. By initiating repair the parent is also showing that she wants her child to feel safe in the relationship. She will not use a threat to safety as a means of trying to change her child's behavior. However important the reasons for the break, the relationship itself is more important. By making such a statement clearly, she is not undermining her authority. If the child's behavior caused the break, the behavior itself may still warrant a consequence, but it never warrants creating doubt about the safety of the relationship.

Parents may think that, while repair is necessary, it should be the child who initiates it if the child's behavior caused the break in the first place. However, it is the behavior, not the relationship, that requires discipline. By accepting responsibility for initiating the repair, the parent is demonstrating that the relationship is separate from the discipline. She is also acknowledging that she is the source of safety for her child, not vice versa. She will assume any responsibility needed to ensure that the relationship remains healthy. She will make clear to the child the importance of their relationship, even more so if they disagree regarding issues of discipline. If she insists that her child is responsible for initiating repair, she is communicating that he is responsible for the continuity of the relationship. Since that is not his responsibility, he is likely to interpret his parent's failure to initiate repair as representing little or no intention to do so. He might think that the relationship is not that important to her. He will feel less safe and will be unlikely to have the confidence to take the first step. A downward spiral of negative distancing may emerge in their relationship. Even if he does initiate repair, he is likely to experience resentment that he had to be good and be sorry before his parent would welcome him again into her mind and heart.

Third, initiating repair does not reinforce any behaviors of the child that might be related to the break. Attachment security is an unconditional goal of appropriate parenting. Safety should never be a reward that we have to earn.

Some parents might be concerned that while reinforcement is not the goal, it may be an unintended side effect. This is not likely if the parents provide closeness throughout the day and week. When the parent and child are routinely safe and engaged with each other, the child is not led to initiate a break in order to achieve repair, since the closeness that repair facilitates is what he already possesses.

Finally, as I have stressed throughout this work, there is no value in trying to deliberately create insecurity in a child's attachment with his parents. Many studies have shown in many areas that secure attachment is associated with healthy development throughout childhood and into adulthood. Creating insecurity places the child at some risk that these developmental gains either will not occur or will not be so large. Beyond that, lacking attachment security places the child at some risk of various developmental problems that might best be avoided. It will not facilitate healthy independence and self-reliance. Rather, it may create a rigid avoidance of others while trying to manage situations alone that are best managed in the company of trusted family and friends. Or it may create a child so focused on trying to achieve security that he gives less attention to his own needs for autonomy.

Attachment-Focused Dialogue

In the following example, John and his mother have a conflict which leads to them both becoming angry and John running to his room. Later, John's mother initiates a repair, not as an apology, but as a clear statement that the relationship is very important and she will repair it whenever there has been a break, regardless of the cause of the break.

> *Mom*: John, I'm not going to buy you that video game. I know that it is important to you, but I don't think that it is a good use of your time, nor your mind.
>
> *John*: But Rick has one, Mom, and it's a great game! Just lend me the money now and I'll pay you back with my allowances.
>
> *Mom*: John, that's not the point. You can't get it, money or not. I really do not like the content of that game! I don't want your mind in that violence for hours.
>
> *John*: Mom, I'm 15! It's a new century! Guys my age play those games all the time!
>
> *Mom*: I do know the century we're in, John. And you're the only 15-year-old I have to look out for.
>
> *John*: I don't need you to look out for me!
>
> *Mom*: The answer is no, John. It's time we stopped discussing this.
>
> *John*: You're just an old lady who doesn't know anything!
>
> *Mom*: I'm your mother, John! [with anger] And I'm not an old lady to you! You can be mad at me, but you can't call me an old lady!
>
> *John*: I am mad at you! Why wouldn't I be! [Runs to his room and slams the door] [Mom is still angry as she finishes opening her mail. As she calms down, she begins preparations for dinner. After about 15 minutes, she feels calm enough to

repair her relationship with her son, and she guesses that he most likely will be calm enough to be responsive. She knocks on his bedroom door, waits a minute, and enters. John is lying on his bed staring at the ceiling.]

Mom: How are you?

John: [Gives no response as he continues to stare at the ceiling]

Mom: We both got kind of mad at each other. We had some big feelings there. I'm doing better now and I was hoping that you might be too.

John: I just don't see why I can't get that game, Mom.

Mom: I know that you don't, John. I know. And I also know that this is important to you.

John: It is, Mom.

Mom: I know. And because of that, I tried to be real sure that my decision was the right one. And I've thought about it and I still believe that it is.

John: I don't get it, Mom. You know I won't go around killing people.

Mom: I know, John. I never thought that you would. And I don't think that your imagination would go naturally in that direction.

John: Then why not, Mom?

Mom: Because your mind is so special to me. I want better for it.

John: It's just a game.

Mom: I know, John, but not a game that I want your mind to spend hours on.

John: [Silence]

Mom: Are you still angry with me?

John: No, Mom. I'm not. Maybe just upset about your decision.

Mom: Anything I can do to help you with it? [smiles and touches his arm]

John: No, Mom. You know that I'm 15. [laughs]

Mom: [Smiles] I know you are, and growing up in front of my eyes. And I'm so proud to be your mom.

John: Me too, Mom.

Mom: I need you to know that it didn't feel good when you
  called me an old lady.

John: I know, Mom. I'm sorry. I didn't mean that.

Mom: You don't think I'm old?

John: Well, you know what I mean.

Mom: What, John?

John: I shouldn't have called you that when I was mad at you.
  I'm sorry I did.

Mom: Apology accepted, John. I'm glad you realize why that
  would bother me.

John: I do, Mom. I really do.

Mom: I'm glad, John. It's important to me that we can be
  angry with each other without calling each other names.

John: I won't, Mom. I get it.

Mom: Of course, the next time that you're angry, you have my
  permission to call me a young woman! [laughs]

John: You got it! [laughs]

CHAPTER TEN

Reducing Attachment Resistance

A child may resist developing attachment security with his parents for a variety of reasons, including the following:

- The child was exposed to abuse, neglect, or abandonment by his biological parents and is now being raised by foster or adoptive parents.
- The child was exposed to multiple caregivers or placements during his first months or years.
- The child experienced significant medical problems during his initial months or years.
- The child had significant prenatal problems that compromised his early attachment-seeking behaviors.
- The child's primary caregivers had their own unresolved attachment history.
- The child's primary caregiver was significantly depressed during his initial months or years.
- The child's primary caregivers manifested significant substance abuse or mental illness during his initial months or years.

In some circumstances, the initial problems that interfered with attachment behaviors may have been minor. However, they may have caused the parent and infant to be out of sync, which in turn caused hesitation and uncertainty on the part of one or both of them. This hesitation may have caused a gradual lack of confidence in one or both, which then led to avoidance of attachment-related interactions. A vicious circle could then ensue that led to a gradual and persistent increase in their difficulty forming attachment security over the following months and years.

Such doubt and lack of confidence might easily lead to a tendency to blame the other—either parent or child—as the source of the relationship difficulties. Gradually, each could begin to assume that the motives of the other were negative (e.g., self-centered, not trying, never satisfied, not caring), which would quickly lead to a lack of intersubjective influence and engagement.

Just as there might be a vicious circle that leads to a worsening of attachment problems, it is also possible to develop a positive cycle in the present that can address attachment problems that originated in the past. Much of the responsibility for initiating this new pattern lies with the parent, rather than the child. If the parent is able to perceive the behavioral and relationship problems from an attachment perspective, she is likely to be able to perceive the inner life of her child in a manner that is inherently hopeful, rather than hopeless. The possible solutions lie in changing the nature of their relationship, increasing the safety provided by the relationship, perceiving the inner life of the child differently, and providing an intersubjective presence that will create these changes, one interactive sequence at a time.

When their lives together can be faced honestly and with commitment, shame and fear begin to dissipate and the events of their lives can be accepted and integrated into their joint history. *Building the Bonds of Attachment* (2006) describes the journey of one very traumatized child toward developing a secure attachment with her preadoptive mother.

Characteristics of Attachment Resistance

Many children who resist turning to their parents for both safety and exploration of self and the world tend to develop similar strategies for self-reliance and coping. These strategies reflect the psychological reality that they are responsible for both their own safety and for learning about the world. They either cannot rely on their parents, are able to but believe that they cannot, or are unable to because of developmental or psychological factors within themselves. As a result, they tend to develop a vigilant control over the events and objects of their lives. They tend to tell others—including their parents—what they are convinced is best and what others should do. They tend to want to decide the best course of action for themselves and to oppose the decisions of their parents and others.

These children also try to avoid any event that might be associated with prior events involving fearful and shameful experiences. They develop a strong avoidance of memories of those prior events as well as any current situations that might elicit those memories. These children, in a fundamental way, may never feel safe since they fear parts of their own mind. Not only are they hypervigilant about external events, they are equally hypervigilant about allowing parts of their inner life to enter awareness. They often react with intense rage or terror when seemingly routine events—associated with past traumas—elicit an intense emotional response. Parents may facilitate perceived safety by controlling what their child is exposed to in the external world. It is much harder for parents to increase their child's sense of safety when his fears originate within himself.

Given that these children have not relied on their attachment figures in any consistent manner, they also are likely not to show the developmental skills that children with attachment security tend to manifest. Their emotional experience and expressions tend toward the extremes, lacking a "thermostat" that will create flexible regulation. Their ability to reflect upon the events of their lives tends to be weak, as they react to situations, often in a repetitive and rigid manner driven by fears regarding safety.

The patterns that they demonstrate often include varying degrees of the following:

1. Pervasive desire to control the events and people in their lives.

2. Difficulty with intersubjective experience and reciprocal communication and influence.
3. Habitual hypervigilance.
4. Emotional volatility involving intense anger, fears, despair, and shame.
5. Emotional numbness.
6. Difficulty anticipating the consequences of the actions of self or others.
7. Pervasive sense of shame involving a sense of being unlovable, worthless, or bad.
8. Some difficulties experiencing empathy for others.
9. Some difficulties perceiving their own inner lives—avoiding the awareness of many memories, thoughts, feelings, and intentions.
10. Some difficulties accurately perceiving the inner lives of others—often assuming negative thoughts, feelings, and motives directed toward them.
11. Possible related difficulties involving speech-language, sensori-motor, and self-care development.
12. Difficulty experiencing a coherent and continuous sense of self, other, and the attachment relationship. Experience tends to be disjointed.

Reducing Attachment Resistance

In their efforts to increase their child's attachment toward them, parents should focus both on the intersubjective quality of the relationship as well as more comprehensive factors in the home environment. The following suggestions address both factors.

Intersubjective

As has been stressed in earlier chapters, intersubjective experience involves reciprocal influence upon each other created by a moment-to-moment engagement during which the parent and child are in joined states of affective rhythm and intensity, awareness, and purpose. Through this shared experience, the experience of each is deepened and made more comprehensive through the experience of the other.

When a parent invites her securely attached child into the inter-subjective dance, the child tends to join with eagerness and delight, or at least with acceptance and interest. If the child resists such a dance periodically, she accepts that decision as reflecting his desire to be psychologically alone for a time, knowing that in the not too distant future, her child will readily join the dance again. She waits at a distance, attending to her own solitary interests as well, and then joins her child when he is ready to do so.

When a child habitually resists such experiences, the parent must consider other options besides waiting until he is ready. He may never be ready. He is likely to need her active presence and persistent initiatives if he is to develop the interest and ability to engage with others intersubjectively.

Such recurring initiatives must not involve threats, anger, power struggles, or rewards and punishments, or they will lose their inter-subjective quality. While the parent needs to initiate the invitation to engage—repeatedly—she needs to do so without forgetting her child's conviction that such experiences are difficult and should be avoided. Her best stance is one of gentle persistence. An attitude of PACE, over an extended period of time, tends to be the most effective approach.

Thus, when a parent takes an intersubjective initiative, her resist-ant child is likely to withdraw, become irritated, argue, become dis-tractible, or completely ignore her initiative. If she accepts his response and responds to it with curiosity, she inviting the resistance into the intersubjective context. She is choosing to experience the resistant response as her child's unique, but limited, way of communicating with her about an aspect of his inner life. That aspect may involve dis-missive thoughts, irritated emotions, withdrawing intentions, or neg-ative perceptions about her inner life. She is responding with PACE, because she believes that his behavior-in part-indicates that he does want to engage with his mother.

She responds to his communication of his subjective experience at that moment. Her message is: "Though I might have wanted to talk with you about baking a pie, I am equally interested in taking your lead and sharing your experience of wanting me to leave you alone. Help me to understand that experience." In this example, the mother's message is that sharing experience intersubjectively is her goal. She is not invested in sharing only certain experiences (e.g., fun, successes, interests). She wants to know any aspect of her son's experience, and if his experience often involves a desire to be left alone, she is most interested in understanding that experience since it occurs frequently in his life. Her curiosity might lead to empathy ("I wonder if it is ever hard for you having to carry so much of your thoughts by yourself") or playfulness ("Getting that response when I asked you to bake a pie with me makes me glad that I didn't ask you to help with the dishes"). Underneath the entire sequence, however, is her acceptance that this is his experience in the moment and she is willing to engage with him intersubjectively around whatever subjective experience he has.

The following alternative responses are probably not going to be successful:

1. Waiting until he decides to initiate an intersubjective engagement. That wait may last years.
2. Withdrawing in discouragement and resentment when he rejects her initiative.
3. Giving a lecture that he should respond, being motivated by gratitude or obligation.
4. Asking him why he is refusing her initiative. Being frustrated with his answer or lack of an answer.

The following sequence might produce better results:

Mom: Hey, Bob, how about baking a pie with me? I don't think that I ever showed you how to do it and it might come in handy someday.
Bob: Get real!
Mom: I'm real already, Bob. It's the pie that I want to get real.
Bob: Funny!
Mom: Okay. Maybe that was a bit lame. But what's going on? You seem annoyed with me for asking. What's that about?

Bob: That's just stupid—baking a pie. Like I really want to do that.

Mom: I thought it was a bit of a stretch for you since I never heard you express any interest in baking. So, I'm fine with your not wanting to bake it. I'm still curious, though, about why you're annoyed with me for asking.

Bob: You should know that I wouldn't want to do it.

Mom: Oh, Okay. You're saying that you're annoyed because I didn't know that you would never be interested in baking a pie.

Bob: Yeah, you don't know me at all.

Mom: Oh, Okay. Now it makes more sense. You're saying that my asking you means that I just don't know you very well. That I haven't taken the time to get to know you.

Bob: Yeah. Why would you think that I would want to bake a pie?

Mom: I can't say that I did think that, Bob. I really didn't know, but since I was baking one, I thought that I would ask you.

Bob: Yeah.

Mom: But you're telling me that you wished that I hadn't because you're losing confidence in me. You think that I don't know you very well after all and maybe even that I'm not that interested in getting to know you.

Bob: Well, do you? Do you want to get to know me?

Mom: With all my mind and heart, Bob. But what's important is that you don't think that I want to. It might seem to you that you're not important to me if it seems that I'm not really interested in getting to know you. That I just make assumptions about you but don't really know you.

Bob: You assumed that I wanted to bake a pie!

Mom: Somehow that's where we were out of sync, Bob. I wasn't aware of assuming that. I was aware of wanting to do something original with you. And maybe even finding out if you might have a small interest in baking. I think that my question was more a desire to get to know you better rather than how you experienced it, which was that it showed ignorance about you and no interest in getting to know you.

Since that was your experience, I think that I have to do a
better job of expressing my purpose. Would you help me
with that?

Bob: What?

Mom: When it seems that I have made a judgment about you
without trying to get to know your experience, would you
tell me that or else ask me what my purpose for asking is?

Bob: I guess.

Mom: Great. I think that will help us get to know each other
better.

The suggestion that the parent accept the child's resistance to intersubjective dialogue is definitely easier said than done. By the very
nature of intersubjectivity, the parent will be influenced by her child's
resistance. It will be hard not to experience the resistance as a rejection. Even though understanding the reasons for the rejection can
minimize its impact, continual resistance can wear most of us down.
The parent needs to constantly remember how the child's inner life
leads him to turn away from the very experience that he truly
needs—the intersubjective presence of his parents that creates both
safety and a coherent sense of self. Perceiving the shame and fear
that underlies the resistant behavior can guide her response toward
providing the playfulness, acceptance, curiosity, and empathy that
he needs.

At times, such reflection is not quite enough. Then the parent
needs to be able to turn to another adult who will help her to maintain perspective as well as energy and confidence. Her partner, best
friend, or possibly a therapist might be crucial in helping her to continue to provide the type of relationship with her child that he needs.
By receiving acceptance, curiosity, and empathy from someone who
can act as her attachment figure, she will be more able to provide the
same qualities to her child.

Environmental

A child who has not developed attachment security with his parents has a difficult time experiencing safety in his day-to-day life. He

habitually relies on himself for safety and he needs to remain hyper-vigilant and persistently controlling. If a parent is to encourage him to begin to rely on her for safety, she is likely to have to first attend to his day-to-day life in detail. If his external environment can gradually help him to feel safe, then he may reduce his self-reliance and begin to rely on his parents. The external environment thus will serve as a stepping stone between turning to a self and turning to a parent for safety.

The following sections discuss central characteristics of such an environment.

Provide Structure for the Day

Free time tends to be "anxiety time" and cause a dysregulation of emotion, thought, and behavior. The routine needs to provide a variety of events that are considered to be central to the child's development. These include active and quiet activities, interactive and solitary activities, play, and appropriate chore-related activities. Any chores are likely to require the active participation of his parents, as his self-directed behavior is likely to be minimal. For this degree of structure to be effective, the intent of the parent needs to be to offer a gift to her child, not give him a punishment. She is giving him this structure because he failed to experience environmental safety when younger and this will provide him with that experience. He does not have to earn any of the activities that are in his scheduled routine. They are being provided because they are good and necessary for him to experience, not because he earned them.

Reduce Choices

When a child habitually does not feel safe, he often becomes very anxious when he has to choose between two or more objects or events. He obsesses about what is the best choice, has little confidence in his choice, and tends to regret his choice a few minutes after making it. When he has many choices, he spends his days jumping back and forth across the fence because the grass is always greener on the other side. When his parents make his choice for him, he often settles into the event with much greater contentment. Initially he may be oppositional about his parents' choosing for him, but when he begins to experience less anxiety and more enjoyment, his opposition tends to dissipate.

Give Gentle Supervision

First, supervision provides a child with a sense of safety through basic physical proximity. A child with difficulties relying on his parents often becomes anxious when a parent is not nearby, even though he is not aware of the reason for his anxiety. Often the disorganizing effect of being alone creates much more dysregulation. Negative attention seeking is also possible, generally without awareness. Second, supervision prevents him from having the choice of whether or not to follow the schedule. When alone, he is often likely to lack the intent to follow it. Having to choose repeatedly whether or not to keep the schedule, he becomes anxious and is likely to impulsively do something different. To be effective, supervision, like structure, needs to be presented with a positive attitude rather than as a negative consequence for misbehavior. It is a gift, not a punishment. Also, supervision does not mean that the parent is interacting with her child all day. She is simply near him and aware of him, and he is aware of her protective and guiding presence.

Have Family Rituals

The parents should have clear and frequent family rituals that make it evident that the child is a member of the family and that he is claimed by his parents as their child. The rituals are part of the daily, weekly, and yearly schedules. Examples of such rituals might include: reading a favorite line from a book before dinner, Thursday evening popcorn and video night, Sunday afternoon explorations of the city, or preparing a meal for the whole family together every other Saturday. They provide continuity of his place in the family. They encourage the development of his attachment as a central part of his identity. With patience and empathy, the child's active participation in these rituals is calmly, firmly expected.

Facilitate Success

Without attachment security, a child is less likely to turn to his parents for guidance regarding how to be successful. He is also less likely to acknowledge his mistakes and try to correct them. He is less likely to communicate his difficulties and ask for help. As a result, he is not likely to learn from his mistakes and so correct them. Rather, he is more likely to make the same mistake again and again. This most likely will create a pervasive sense of failure. Rather than ask for help, he is likely to rely on himself more, become even more hypervigilant and controlling. With structure, supervision, and limited choices, his environment makes success more likely and failure more difficult. Until he can learn from his mistakes, they have to be kept to a minimum by his environment.

There are different reasons why children who resist attachment have trouble learning from their mistakes. First, their pervasive sense of shame causes them to deny mistakes, have excuses for them, or blame others. Second, they often have developmental difficulties that place them in situations that that they are not prepared for. They tend to be raised or taught at school according to their chronological age rather than their developmental age. Basic skills of self-direction, impulse control, frustration tolerance, and delay of gratification tend to be weak, leaving them at high risk for failure in many situations.

Give Time-In, Not Time-Out

Rather than isolating her child when he is misbehaving, the parent brings him closer to her. She increases his physical proximity in order to provide a background of safety rather than generating anxiety through isolation. Parents intuitively do this when their child is frightened or sad. They tend to forget it when their child is angry. A parent's goal in keeping her child closer is not to interact with him. Rather, her calm and confident presence will have a contagious effect on his emotional distress. She is aware of him in her periphery, just as he is aware of her. Gradually as he calms, she tentatively reaches out to soothe him. When a parent is routinely available and interactive with her child during the day, soothing him during hard times does not reinforce bad behavior.

When a parent withdraws not physically but psychologically, the anxiety may be even more difficult for the child to manage. When he is near her and he can tell that she is not willing to engage with him intersubjectively, he is certain to feel isolation and rejection. Even if she is not speaking with him, he is able to tell from her nonverbal expressions that her mind and heart—her thoughts and emotions—are withdrawn from him and she is experiencing him negatively. When the parent is not ready to reengage with her child, she is wise to give herself a time-out, explaining in a matter-of-fact manner that she needs some time to calm down and she will be available for him shortly. When the child needs supervision, ideally another adult will be present when she needs her time-out.

Some children, due to shame, have difficulty remaining in the presence of their parents when there is a conflict. They should be allowed to calm down in another room if they choose, but not be forced to be isolated. When calm, it is important to repair the relationship as soon as possible. Forcing relationship repair before the child is ready to be somewhat engaged is likely only to reescalate the situation.

Initiate Soothing

A child who wants to rely on himself tends to resist being soothed by his parent because he knows that he is likely to rely on her more if he accepts soothing from her. She can soothe with a gentle, empathic word or eye gaze. She soothes when she gently touches or strokes her child for a moment or for as long as he can comfortably tolerate. She stops the soothing behavior when she senses that her child is about to become uncomfortable rather than after he begins to be. When he says, "Leave me alone," she accepts that without sensing rejection. She knows that it comes from fear. She respects his desire that she stop, and she is ready to do it again the next time he is in distress. Soothing might be given psychologically, if not physically, when her child is very resistant to it. She might say, "I think that you need a hug, but I can see that you do not want me to hug you now. I respect that, so I'll hug you in my mind." She might then close her eyes and smile quietly. If he is bothered by that, she might say, "I know it's hard to watch me hugging you, even when it is in my mind, so I'll do it in the other room." She might hug a stuffed animal that represents her child until he is able to accept it himself. Many children can accept these transitional approaches to actual hugs.

Safeguard Sleep

A child with attachment resistance is likely to be hypervigilant throughout the day. He lives being overtired and still has trouble transitioning into the sleep cycle, if only because of the loss of control that will follow. To facilitate a more successful sleep routine, the parent may have to start his bedtime routine a few hours prior to his actual bedtime. During this time, the schedule needs to be very predictable, with little stimulation or excitement. As bedtime approaches, one-to-one time tends to be the most successful. Activities are quiet and predictable and provide soothing to the extent that he will accept them. Telling and reading stories, listening to music, touch including backrubs, reviewing the day, or anticipating the next day's activity might be helpful. Having a waking-up ritual may help the child who fears that the nighttime separation will lead to loss. Allowing the child to take one of his parent's sweaters with him to bed may also reduce his fears of loss. The bedroom itself needs to be mindfully planned. Its location, size, objects in the room, and presence of sounds and lights all need to be considered. The child's input regarding stuffed animals, posters, relaxing music, and the types and locations of nightlights might make all the difference. One child asked for an aquar-ium and he immediately slept much better because of the blue light, bubbling sounds, and moving fish.

Safeguard a Positive Family Atmosphere

The child with attachment difficulties is likely to frequently experience negative emotions such as anger, fear, and shame. It is important that these emotions not have a contagious effect on the rest of the family. Reacting in kind to the child's negative emotional states creates a vicious circle that is hard to change. It is crucial to respond to the vulnerabilities and strengths that underlie the child's symptoms and problems rather than reacting to the behaviors themselves. The challenge is for the parent to maintain a positive affective tone that might influence her child, rather than letting her child's negative tone influence her.

Protect Against Overstimulation

The child with attachment difficulties is likely to be easily overstimulated. Noise and novelty, unpredictability and change are likely to be experienced as dysregulating rather than interesting. Lacking an effective emotional thermostat, the child is likely to react to environmental changes with extreme emotional swings rather than more moderate, regulated emotions. It is easy to overestimate how much stimulation children with regulation problems can tolerate. When there is a sudden deterioration in the child's functioning, the first question that his parent might ask is: "Does he feel unsafe?" And the second question: "Is he overstimulated?"

Be Securely Attached Yourself

The parent of a child with attachment resistance will be able to address and respond best to his pervasive needs if her own attachment history is resolved. If not, resolution needs to be a priority. Professional intervention may be helpful, if not necessary. Even if her attachment history is resolved, she still may benefit from having an attachment figure to rely on if she is to meet the intense needs of her child for a long period of time.

Attachment-Focused Dialogue

Ron, age 9, was an angry boy who frequently defied his mother, often in sneaky ways. His mother, a single parent, had been abusing alcohol for much of his first 4 years, often neglecting to ensure his safety through adequate supervision and providing for his basic needs. Since then, she had actively participated in a substance abuse treatment program that included addressing her depression and failed parental responsibilities.

A therapist, Mark, had established an initial relationship with Ron and his mother and had become aware that the mother's alcohol abuse during Ron's first 4 years was still impacting his functioning. Mark scheduled a joint session between Ron and his mother to help Ron understand the origins of his current behavior problems as well as developing safety within the mother-son relationship. He had previously spoken with Ron's mother alone in order to be confident that she would be able to address her past difficulties with her son. Because of the significant progress that she made in her own treatment, she felt safe enough to assist her son by acknowledging her failures with him.

Mark: Ron, now we're going to talk about some things that might be kind of hard for you. If you want a break at any time, just let us know and we'll take one. Okay?

Ron: Yeah, let's take one now. [laughs]

Mark: Now! Nice try! You have to wait at least 5 minutes.

Ron: Okay.

Mom: Ron, rather than talking about the conflicts you and I are having now, Mark and I think it would be helpful if we talked today about that long time when you were little when I used to drink all the time. I really did not take care of you very well then.

Ron: [Looks questioningly at his mother]

Mom: First, I want to tell you how sorry I am for all that I've done and not done that has made your life so difficult. I am very, very sorry, Ron.

Ron: I know, Mom. You don't have to talk about that.

Mom: I know. And I've said it before, but I can never say it enough. I am sorry! Second, I want to tell you that none of it was your fault. I treated you poorly when you were little, not because of how you were acting but because of my own problems, especially my drinking. Not because you were bad in any way.

Ron: You used to say that it was my fault that you drank.

Mom: Oh, Ron, I'm so sorry that I said that. I was wrong. It was not your fault. I never should have said that to you. I was blaming you for my problem that I was not ready to admit and stop.

Ron: Why didn't you try to stop?

Mom: I think that I did try, Ron, but if I did it was not hard enough. I do know that I did not stop . . . and I hurt you a lot . . . and I'm very sorry for that.

Ron: Didn't you want to be my mom?

Mom: Oh, honey, I wanted to be your mom so much . . . so very much, even when I was doing a poor job of it. I think I wanted to so much that when I began to see how much I was messing it up, I just lied to myself and said that I was doing okay, that you were okay, or that it was someone else's fault. I lied to myself and said that I was what I so wanted to be—a good mom to you . . . your good mom.

Ron: I thought it was my fault that you didn't take care of me.

Mom: I know you did, Ron. I know you did. I am so sorry . . . so very sorry that you blamed yourself for everything that I did wrong. That must have made it even worse for you . . . to think that somehow you were bad and deserved how I hurt you so much . . . and you thought it was your fault. I let you think that by not telling you that it was my fault, and especially by not changing . . . not becoming the mom that you needed.

Ron: I still sometimes think that if I had been different that you could have taken better care of me.

Mom: You've been blaming yourself for my behavior for so long, I can certainly understand why you would have a hard time stopping that. I am sorry, Ron. I am sorry that you still think that way about my not taking care of you. I hope that someday you will understand that it was all my fault, not yours, and that will help you to feel better, to know better what a special person you are. And when that day comes I will be so happy for you and proud for you . . . that you did not let my hurting you make you still think that you're bad.

Ron: But you're not bad, Mom.

Mom: Thanks, Ron . . . thanks so much for thinking that about me. Sometimes I think that I am—for hurting you so much . . . for being such a poor mom for you when you were little. I know that what I did . . . my behavior . . . I can change and

it is not me, but sometimes I don't really feel that.
Sometimes I blame me a lot and don't like myself at all.

Ron: Just like I do.

Mom: Just like you do . . . so maybe that's something we can
both work on. You did nothing. There is nothing about you
that would cause you to deserve how I treated you . . .
nothing. It was my actions that were wrong, and I can
change them. I am changing them. I can . . . I will be the
mom that you need me to be. I can . . . I will . . . be the
person I want to be.

Ron: But you never hit me. You didn't abuse me like other
kids' moms and dads do.

Mom: I'm proud of that, Ron. No, I never beat you, though I
did hit your bottom sometimes. But I know that I hurt you
in ways that may have hurt your heart and your mind more
than your body. When I looked at you and felt rage at you
for crying or being upset because you were hungry . . .
I'm sure that you saw in my eyes and heard in my voice my
rage . . . my blaming you . . . and you probably felt bad and
scared. And other times I know hurt you a lot. Times when
you just wanted to play with me . . . or sit in my lap . . . or
have me cuddle with you and read you a story at bedtime,
and I yelled no or "leave me alone." Ron, those times, I
know, hurt you a lot . . . a very lot. You must have felt that I
did not love you . . . that you were not special to me . . . that
you deserved how I treated you. That's what I'm sorry for,
Ron, and I'll always regret it.

Ron: It's okay, mom.

Mom: I robbed you of those years, when you were so tiny, and
could have felt happy and loved and safe and special to
me . . . and you didn't I'll always be sorry that you did not
have that . . . and that I did not have those times
with you.

Ron: We can now, Mom.

Mom: Yes, we can, and we will. And these times . . . that we
are going to have together will be some of the most happy
times of my life.

Ron: And mine, too, Mom.

Another Attachment-Focused Dialogue

Frequently, foster and adopted children who have been traumatized by their biological parents have significant difficulty forming a secure attachment with their new parents. They show an extreme need to be in control of all events and people. They have no confidence that their new parents will place their best interests first, and they do not turn to them for comfort and safety. Dialogue like the following is likely to be common in such situations.

In this dialogue, 12-year-old Jean, adopted three years earlier, is reacting with intense anger at her adoptive mother's routine limit setting. Her mother has received considerable professional guidance and support to understand Jean's very disorganized inner life and attachment patterns as well as to communicate with her in a manner that might facilitate conflict resolution and repair.

> *Jean*: I just hate you so much! You never let me do anything! Never!
>
> *Mom*: I get how mad you are! I really do! But are you sure that hate is the right word?
>
> *Jean*: I do hate you! I do! Why wouldn't I, the way you treat me!
>
> *Mom*: Wait a second! What are you talking about? How do I treat you?
>
> *Jean*: How do you think? You never let me do what I want!
>
> *Mom*: Okay! I think i'm getting it. It seems to you that I really never let you do what you want.
>
> *Jean*: That's what I said! And it's true!
>
> *Mom*: Wait! If you're right, why would I never let you do what you want? What would be my reason?
>
> *Jean*: I don't know! You tell me!
>
> *Mom*: But what do you think—If I never let you do what you want—What would be my reason?
>
> *Jean*: I don't know! Maybe you want me to be miserable!
>
> *Mom*: Wow! If that's right, no wonder you'd be mad at me. But why would I want you to be miserable?
>
> *Jean*: Because you hate me, okay?

Mom: Oh my! How hard that must feel, if you think that I hate you!

Jean: You do! But so what? That's how it always is! I'm not surprised!

Mom: Oh, Jean! You expect me to hate you! You think that I do and you're not surprised. I'm so sorry that you see it that way.

Jean: But it's true! It always has been! Don't you get it?

Mom: Help me to understand. Why do you think it always seems that no one cares, that everyone hates you?

Jean: Because that's who I am and that's what I deserve! Are you happy now?

Mom: Not happy, oh, no! Very sad, very sad that you think you deserve to be hated. Very sad . . . very sad.

Jean: Why do you care? Why are you different?

Mom: Because I see parts of you that you don't see. Because I love parts of you that you don't love.

Jean: What are you talking about?

Mom: I'm talking about my daughter, the girl under the problems, under the anger. The girl, my girl, who never was discovered until you came here.

Jean: Discovered.

Mom: Yeah, who you were when you were born, waiting to be seen and loved. Well, honey, you waited 9 years till you met me.

Jean: Like you've never been mad at me.

Mom: The first year was hard, honey. I didn't see you very well. Your anger and your fighting me every step made me think that was you. I didn't know how to see who you were under all that, under all the fighting . . . and I didn't see how the fighting was what you had to do all those years thinking that no one cared, that everyone hated you . . . and probably many did. I'm so sorry, honey.

Jean: So why did they hate me if I'm so special?

Mom: I don't know why your first parents hurt you so bad. But I do know that no baby, no 1-, 2-, 3-year-old child deserves what they did to you. I know that. And you had to fight to live, and some of your foster parents only saw your fighting and probably did start to think that you were bad under your anger. And I didn't understand at first, but I do now. I really do. I see who you are under your fighting and I want you to trust me that you don't have to keep fighting me so much. That's what I want more than anything in the world.

Jean: Why do you want that?

Mom: Because you're my daughter. Because you're so special to me. Because I do know parts of you that you don't see. And because I do love you so much.

Jean: And if I keep hating you when you won't give me what I want?

Mom: I'll keep loving you, and maybe get mad at times. I'll keep trying to get you to see who I am under my behavior that says no to you. Why I say no to you.

Jean: Why do you?

Mom: I say no when I believe that something is not good for you. I only want what I think is best for you, and sometimes we disagree, but my reasons are good.

Jean: Yeah, we often disagree.

Mom: Maybe we will disagree less as we know each other more . . . as you trust me more. As you trust that I'm right about what I know about you.

Jean: You better be patient.

Mom: I am patient with you. Please be patient with me and with yourself.

Jean: It's hard.

Mom: Yes, I know.

REFERENCES

Cassidy, J. (1999). The nature of the child's ties. In J. Cassidy & P. Shaver (Eds.), *Handbook of attachment* (pp. 3–20). New York: Guilford.

Cassidy, J., & Shaver, P. R. (Eds.). (1999). *Handbook of attachment*. New York: Guilford.

Greenberg, M. T. (1999). Attachment and psychopathology in childhood. In J. Cassidy & P. Shaver (Eds.), *Handbook of attachment* (pp. 469–496). New York: Guilford.

Grossmann, K. E., Grossmann, K., & Waters, E. (Eds.). (2005). *Attachment from infancy to adulthood: The major longitudinal studies*. New York: Guilford.

Grossmann, K. E., Grossmann, K., & Zimmermann, P. (1999). A wider view of attachment and exploration: Stability and change during the years of immaturity. In J. Cassidy & P. Shaver (Eds.), *Handbook of attachment* (pp. 760–786). New York: Guilford.

Hughes, D. A. (2006). *Building the bonds of attachment (2nd ed.)*. New York: Jason Aronson.

Hughes, D. A. (2007). *Attachment-focused family therapy*. New York: Norton.

Kabat-Zinn, M. & Kabat-Zinn, J. (1997). *Everyday blessing: The inner work of mindful parenting*. New York: Hyperion.

Lyons-Ruth, K., & Jacobvitz, D. (1999). Attachment disorganization: Unresolved loss, relational violence, and lapses in behavioral and attentional strategies. In J. Cassidy & P. Shaver (Eds.), *Handbook of attachment* (pp. 520–554). New York: Guilford.

Schore, A. N. (2000). Attachment and the regulation of the right brain. *Attachment and Human Development, 2*, 23–47.

Schore, A. N. (2003). *Affect regulation and the repair of the self*. New York: Norton.

Schore, A. N. (2005). Attachment, self regulation, and the developing right brain: Linking developmental neuroscience to pediatrics. *Pediatrics in Review, 26*, 204–211.

Siegel, D. J. (1999). *The developing mind.* New York: Guilford.

Siegel, D. J. (2007). *The mindful brain.* New York: Norton.

Siegel, D. J., & Hartzell, M. (2003). *Parenting from the inside out.* New York: Jeremy P. Tarcher/Putnam.

Sroufe, L. A., Egeland, B., Carlson, E., & Collins, W. A. (2005). *The development of the person.* New York: Guilford.

Tangney, J., & Dearing, R. (2002). *Shame and guilt.* New York: Guilford.

Trevarthen, C. (2001). Intrinsic motives for companionship in understanding: Their origin, development, and significance for infant mental health. *Infant Mental Health Journal, 22*, 95–131.

Trevarthen, C., & Aitken, K. J. (2001). Infant intersubjectivity: Research, theory, and clinical applications. *Journal of Child Psychology and Psychiatry, 42*, 3–48.

INDEX